I0823007

Praise for *Voices of the Herd*

"I've spent time with cows, the rescued and the doomed, and these photos capture the personality of each being—their soul even—in a way I would not have expected in a two-dimensional medium. How Peters managed this is one of those mysteries that, lacking a photographer's talent, I will never understand. I simply know that I want to return again and again to these compelling images and the succinct, moving stories of each rescue."
—**Victoria Moran**, author of *Main Street Vegan* and co-screenwriter of the movie *Miss Liberty*

"Cows are highly intelligent and deeply sentient and emotional beings. Each and every individual has a unique personality, and it's fair to say not a single cow enjoys being farmed for human meals. In *Voices of the Herd*, Mark Peters shares deeply moving and personal photographs and stories of rescued 'food cows'—the fortunate few spared from lives of unimaginable suffering. Through the heartfelt care of compassionate humans, these individuals find safety, love, and healing from their scars of torture and confinement. Reading about Lucky, Moksha, and Watson, to name a few whose stories are told, I was reminded that the right question isn't 'What's for dinner?' but 'Who's for dinner?' I hope this book inspires readers to honor the voices of farmed and rescued cows, who express far more than a simple 'moo,' and rethink the anonymous and hidden lives behind steak, beef, and burgers."—**Marc Bekoff**, Ph.D, author of *The Animals' Agenda: Freedom, Compassion, and Coexistence in the Human Age* and *The Emotional Lives of Animals: A Leading Scientist Explores Animal Joy, Sorrow, and Empathy—and Why They Matter*

"*Voices of the Herd* features striking photographs and poignant stories of cows who have been fortunate enough to escape the horrible fate that befalls tens of millions of their peers in the United States. Photographer Mark Peters' portraits capture the beauty of these souls who share our desire to live."—**Seth Goldman**, co-founder of Eat the Change/ Just Ice Tea, chair of the board of PLNT Burger

“Thank you, Mark Peters, for giving us the rare opportunity to see and get to know beautiful bovines. People don’t know what interesting animals they are! Mark breaks the mold of what animal photography can be and which species we believe to be deserving of portraits, stories, research, and our compassion. Cows are all around us—in crowded farms, on our plates—and we rarely get to see or know them. Mark helps correct that through this collection of stunning portraits and moving stories.”—**Jo-Anne McArthur**, photojournalist and founder of We Animals

“This book is an all-around beauty. With exquisite black-and-white photographs, lyrical prose, and touching stories, Mark Peters presents the true nature of cows in ways that the purveyors of dairy and beef don’t want you to see—as social, sensitive individuals who treasure their lives.”—**Jonathan Balcombe**, author of *Super Fly* and *What a Fish Knows*

“Joy, kindness, playfulness, resilience after trauma—so many cow emotions come alive in this gorgeous book. Peters’ photographs splendidly pair with essays from sanctuary caretakers to highlight cow personalities and love shared among cow family and friends. Everything about this book resonates with me, especially its message motivating us to bring about a kinder world for all beings.”—**Barbara J. King**, author of *How Animals Grieve*

“Filled with exquisite photographs and heart-touching stories, *Voices of the Herd* reveals cows as they really are: very sensitive and very social. The expressions of these cows, joyously living out their lives in sanctuaries, filled me with hope. With its priceless imagery, this book shows us how every cow should be allowed to live . . . in peace.”—**Jane Velez-Mitchell**, *New York Times* bestselling author, UnchainedTV founder

VOICES OF THE HERD

Portraits of Rescued Cows and Their Sanctuary Stories

Mark Peters

Lantern Publishing & Media • Woodstock and Brooklyn, NY

2025
Lantern Publishing & Media
PO Box 1350
Woodstock, NY 12498
www.lanternpm.org

Printed in the United States of America

Library of Congress Cataloging-in-Publication Data is available upon request.

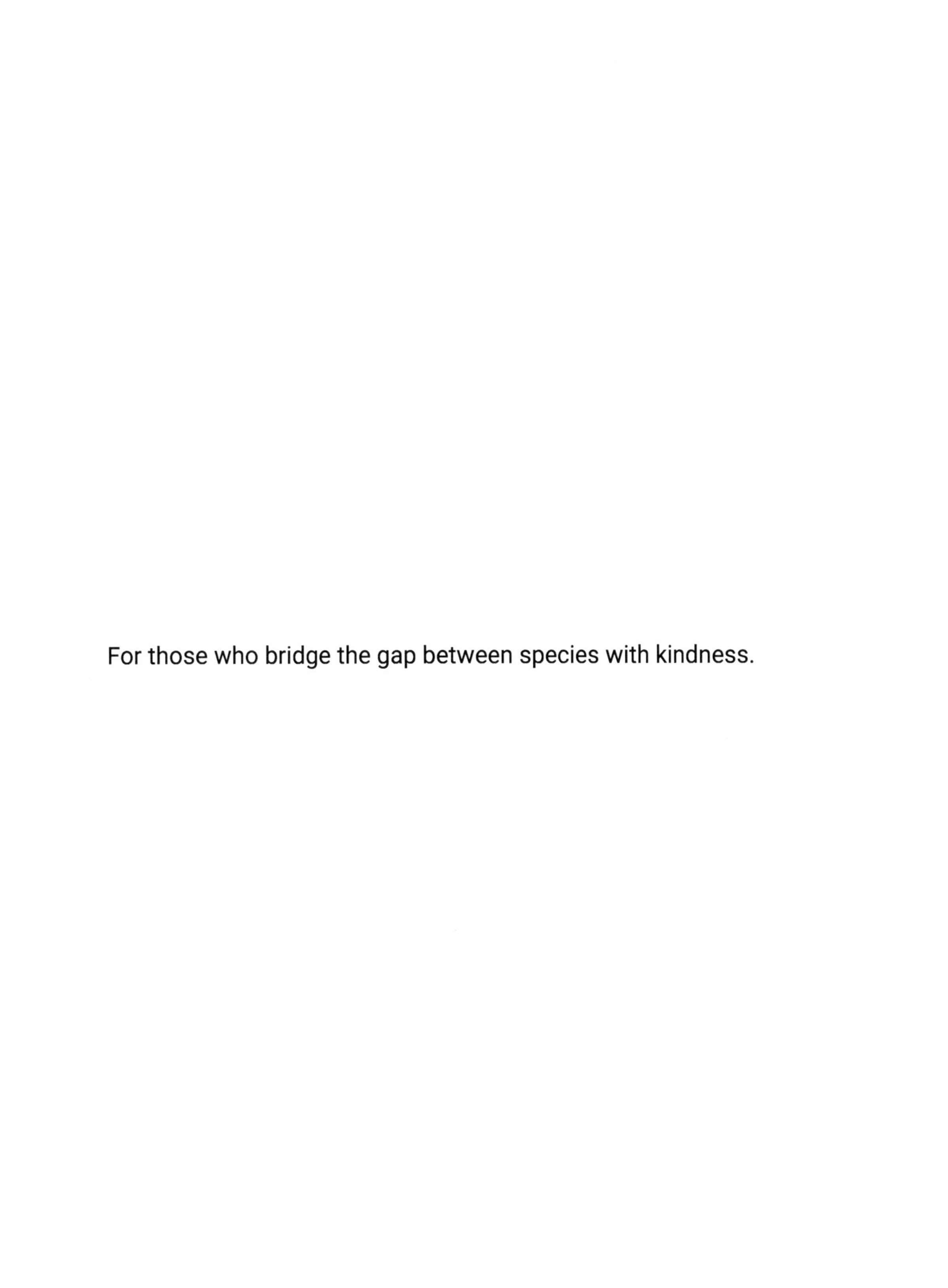

For those who bridge the gap between species with kindness.

CONTENTS

INTRODUCTION

The gate latches behind me in the early morning darkness. I rub my hands together to warm them, then return to my car and roll forward down the winding lane to the sanctuary parking area. After hiking for more than a mile across fields and woods, with the dry autumn grass crackling softly under my boots, I climb a hill, from which I spot them in the distance. My heart thumps with joy. Laughter shreds my frosty breath into bursts of confetti.

Hundreds of acres of land are accessible to the cows to roam. They make fair use of it. When I arrive in the mornings to take advantage of the soft light for photographs, the herd often makes me search across multiple pastures and sometimes into the woods for them.

The sun's glow seeping over the hills illuminates a sweeping parcel of land where the herd had evidently spent the night. At the far end, my friend Remi, a Holstein heifer less than a year old, with a pink nose and knobby knees, forages alongside a much larger steer near the edge of some woods. An observer might not notice that Remi is blind. She was born with no eyesight on a small dairy farm. Taking pity, the farmers contacted the sanctuary to ask if they could accommodate her. Most of the year, she moves within the atomic structure of the herd like an electron, pulled toward the nucleus of activity but unafraid to graze on her own on the far periphery. Remi hears the rustling of her party as it treads across the turf. If she falls behind, a member of her bovine village gives her a gentle nudge on her rump.

As she walks, Remi tilts her head from side to side, snorting plumes of steam while apparently listening to the sounds around her. When she hears a familiar voice, she stands still, excited, her ears pointing upward. After calling Remi's name and gently touching her neck to let her know I was there, I wrap my arms around her and lay my head on her velvety soft back.

Have you ever hugged a cow? You really should. Time shared with cows is generally serene. The resting state of a cow chewing their cud is meditative calm. No expectations, no judgment. Cows fill our arms with their enormous warmth; their tranquil spirit transferred into the soul through touch. Moreover, it's simply delightful to make the acquaintance of a fellow creature with whom we all share the breath of life; to acquaint ourselves with them as beings worthy of loving kindness; and to awaken a sense of wonder when we meet them on their own terms.

Note that I say *cows* rather than *cattle*—a term associated with the animals as property rather than as individuals free to explore natural lives. I also avoid the term *farm animals*, which implies an intrinsic property of the animals themselves, instead favoring *farmed animals*, a condition that is forced upon the individuals born into the intensive agricultural system. The terms we use are important: They shape and reinforce our views of the world.

Like many people, for most of my life I considered myself an animal lover. In practice, this affection applied to the animals whom I got to know—dogs and cats, mostly, and animals praised for their intelligence, like monkeys and dolphins. Beyond these limited species, my love grew more abstract and subject to my whims. I assumed that animals raised for food were somehow lesser, their sole purpose to serve as sustenance for humans. They couldn't have as much whirling around in their noggins as our companion animals. After all, that was the message conveyed in advertising and confirmed by the choices made by people and institutions I admired. I felt a vague sympathy for "livestock" animals but not much else. It wasn't until my forties that I grew to know cows, pigs, chickens, goats, and sheep.

When we began dating, my wife introduced me to Poplar Spring Animal Sanctuary during their open house event, where the pigs followed us around, nudged our pockets and bags in hopes of finding treats and, if rubbed in the right spot, rolled over for belly rubs. The sanctuary staff allowed visitors to hold some of the more receptive chickens, warm in their downy feathers. If you listened closely, you could feel them purr almost like kittens. From that experience onward, I stopped seeing farmed animals as different from other domesticated animals—dogs from pigs, chickens from cats, cows from horses. From what I could tell, there were no significant differences in the species. In all of them, I observed individual beings with wants and needs.

Over ten years of visits to farmed animal sanctuaries, I've watched the resident cows adjust to their new reality: spaciousness versus confinement; fresh air and sunlight versus the darkness of a dirty stall; love and kindness versus abuse, neglect, or indifference. With patience and time, each reveals the secrets deep in their bovine heart.

With rare exceptions, most residents in a farmed animal sanctuary are survivors of abuse. They come from insecure and often precarious systems that curtail or ignore their nature and well-being. They are often broken from physical and mental trauma, victims of a broken trust between an animal and their caregiver. Animals remember how people have treated them; it's a wonder when they open themselves to renewed trust. Sanctuary workers flip the script on their old lives by introducing rescued animals to a world in which they matter and enclosing them like a hug in fencing to keep them safe from harm.

This morning, more cows rise from sleep to begin their day, stretch, and relieve themselves before sniffing the ground for forage. As a courtesy, I approach and scratch their backs or rub their necks when they pause, and step back when they show an inclination to eat.

During sanctuary visits, I note how each cow reacts to being approached on a given day. While working on this book project, I spent hours with the cows in each farmed animal sanctuary over multiple visits, gaining their trust. When photographing subjects who are comfortable with people, I used a wide-angle lens and moved in close. When observing the interactions between herd members or individuals simply being themselves, off on their own, a telephoto lens allowed me to keep my distance and enjoy the natural interplay of behaviors and emotions I witnessed.

When everyone has gained their feet and stooped to feast on grass, I stand aside and watch my friends with appreciation. They spread out and forage across the fields while moving forward, ever forward.

For millions of years, the aurochs, ancestors of modern cows, roamed vast swaths of Europe, Northern Africa, and Asia. Fossil records indicate the auroch bulls stood upwards of six feet at the shoulder, roughly a quarter taller than a Holstein cow, the most prevalent breed used in the dairy industry in the United States and one of the largest cow breeds worldwide. These herbivores were a keystone species within the diverse ecosystems they called home, from savannahs to swamps, from forests to steppes and mountains. From Paleolithic cave drawings to medieval art, the aurochs are portrayed throughout human history with reverence as formidable creatures. Since the Neolithic period (as early as around 10,500 BC), humans simultaneously domesticated wild aurochs (creating the line that led to modern cows) and hunted them for food, ultimately driving them to extinction. The last known aurochs died in 1627 in Poland.

In the fields this morning, Remi grazes alongside her best friend, Grayson, an adolescent steer born to a former dairy cow who arrived pregnant at the sanctuary. They bob along, inevitably wobbling toward each other affectionately like compass needles toward their own magnetic north; Grayson's fawn-colored coat contrasted with Remi's Holstein coloring, white swirls peeking out from behind a wall of blackness. Cows are highly social animals who, when given the chance, form strong bonds with one another. Most herd members graze near and rest beside a preferred cow. Each can sense a friend's reaction of fear or anxiety to an event, and in turn show signs of agitation, even if they haven't experienced the event themselves.[1]

Similar to humans, the typical cow gestation period is nine months. When cows are permitted to raise their calves, they quickly develop strong maternal bonds. The bonding process begins after the birth, when the mother licks and nuzzles her calf clean, and encourages the calf to stand up and nurse. They are loving mothers who protect and nourish their young. Mother cows have been known to hide their calves from farm workers, putting their bodies between unfamiliar vehicles and their calves.[2]

When a mother experiences even a brief separation from her calf after the maternal-filial relationship is established, she displays clear signs of distress: mooing loudly and searching anxiously for her baby. On dairy farms, where calves are taken from their mothers quickly following birth, she bellows longingly for days or even weeks.[3]

Grayson's mother, Maple, is a small tawny cow with strikingly large ebony eyes. When she gave birth to him in the cozy sanctuary barn, she nudged straw over her sleeping calf, trying to hide him from the staff. After seven years of carrying calves to term, only to have them taken from her, Maple had learned to distrust humans. She evidently feared that much the same would happen to this newborn sleeping beside her. The sanctuary staff left mother and calf alone to feel each other's touch, for the baby to suckle and Maple to nuzzle her warm, mewling child, to lick him clean of fluid from his birth and sleep safely together. She was finally free to raise a calf she had carried.

When allowed to remain together, a calf may nurse from their mother for as long as several years. Nursing promotes the mother-calf bond. Long after a calf is weaned, the pair often forage and rest together and, should they wander from each other, reunite and nuzzle each other throughout the day. Mother cows recognize and respond to the voices of their own offspring. Their calves, in turn, know their mom's voice.[4] Their companionship naturally lasts a lifetime.

Within the social network of a familiar herd, other cows help nurture the calves. Cows share "babysitting" duties while the mothers feed and socialize, so that the calves are watched and always protected.[5]

Cows use different pitches of sound to express different needs or emotions. A separated mother and her calf moo to search for each other. Cows moo to say they are hungry, call for a partner when they want to mate, raise an alarm when they sense potential danger, and show contentment or express pain.[6]

As the cows in this sanctuary finish grazing, the momentum of the herd slows. Individuals approach other members of their social group and gently lick their heads, necks, and backs—a practice called grooming. In general, older cows groom younger ones, or the initiator and receiver are of similar age. It's clear that cows lick their herd mates for the same reason chimpanzees groom each other—as a social interaction; to bond.

In 2014, I began to photograph the residents of the Poplar Spring sanctuary after having attended their annual open house and other social events for several years. Among the first cows I came to know were Juliet and Clifford, who arrived around this time. These calves had been rescued from a cruelty case in which they had been kept in chains outdoors with no protection from the heat or thunderstorms and were often denied food and water. As they settled into their new environment, the large Holstein steer and diminutive, auburn Jersey heifer rarely left each other's side. Each seemed to wallow in the tender comfort of the other's presence. They strolled the sanctuary pastures together, as free to wander as the stray breezes that tickled their fuzzy ears. I often lay in the grass and watched them, marveling at their resilience and openness.

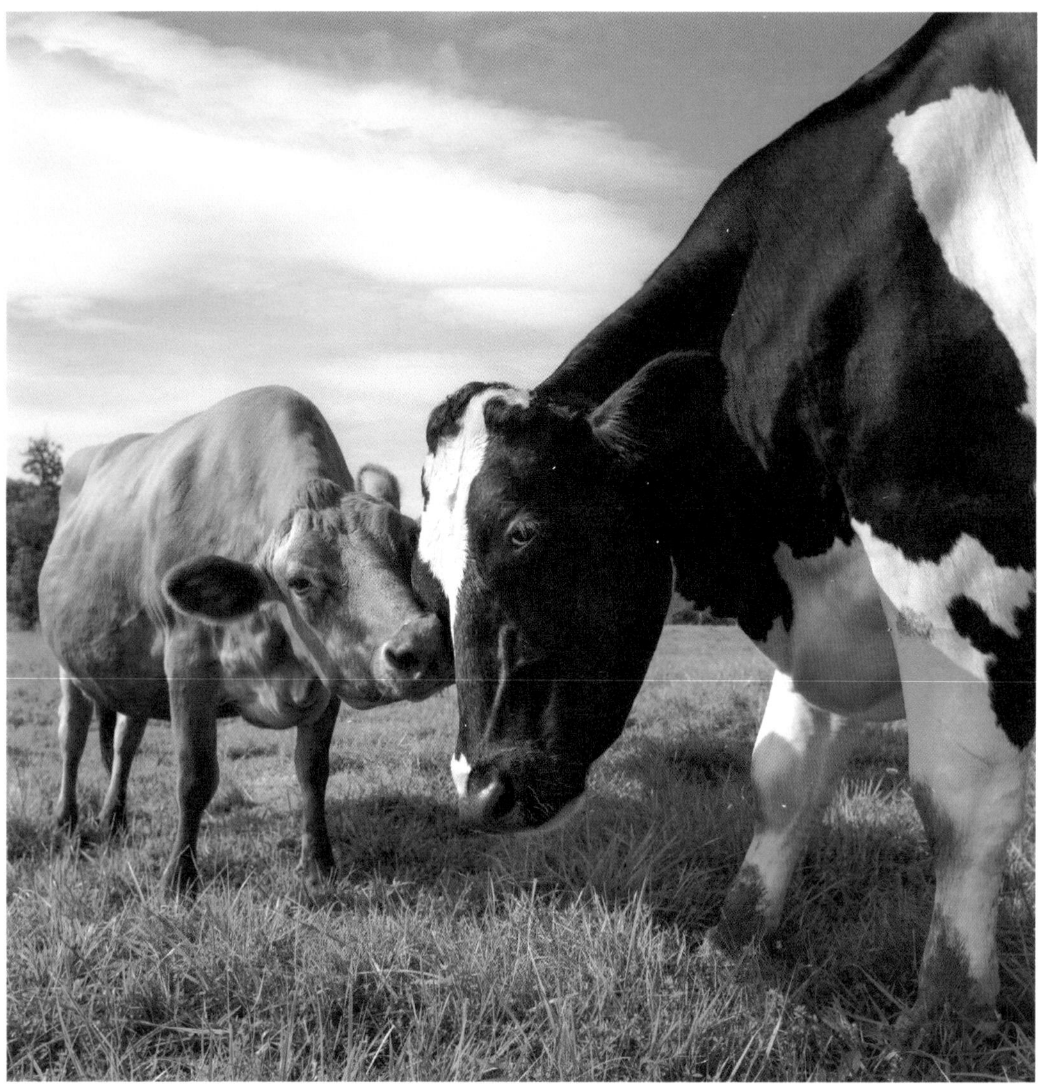

Juliet and Clifford

Some of the individuals featured in this book I've known for upwards of ten years. They're old friends. Others I've known only briefly. All the animals I've met, whether featured here or not, deserve celebration. Aggie was discovered wandering along the railroad tracks near a livestock auction. In a sense, she rescued herself from an uncertain but certainly horrible future. Lucky's mother was attacked by wolves and killed while pregnant with him. Dora Jean was found in a barren field with dozens of starving cows—no edible greenery or water source—surrounded by the bodies of deceased friends and family members. Some of the cows I've photographed have passed on. Their bones lie nestled in the earth, while their essence is released softly into the timeless memories of their mates and the universe, like a diffusion of light.

The cows featured in this book are no different from the millions currently languishing in industrial animal agriculture—fattened for beef in concentrated animal feeding operations (CAFO), also called factory farms, in often filthy and overcrowded feedlots; or, on dairy farms, confined indoors and forced into a repeated cycle of pregnancies. The relative freedom of rescued animals living in a sanctuary environment makes them not exceptional but only exceptionally lucky.

Some of the cows I have met come eagerly to be touched. The loose skin of the neck, called the dewlap, is supple and warm under gentle fingers. More than a few cows have answered my neck rubs by licking my face, which always thrills me to no end. A cow's tongue scrapes rough across the skin, a joyous sensation that can leave surface abrasions but is worth it. Their ruminant breath washes over you, a sweet grassy fragrance.

On this morning, the forward momentum resumes. The herd ambles like the shadow of a cloud over the hills. The movements of individuals suggest no clear destination, a zigzagging coddiwomple, and yet their miles of strolling land them at their troughs near a barn where a staff person serves them supplemental grain for breakfast.

The sanctuaries I visited in the making of this book represent a small fraction of the organizations working tirelessly to rescue animals apportioned the barest of protections, who fall through the cracks in laws of the land. The need greatly outweighs the available space, funding, and human resources. Each year in the United States, approximately 35 million cows are raised for beef, nine million for milk, and 450,000 calves for veal.[7]

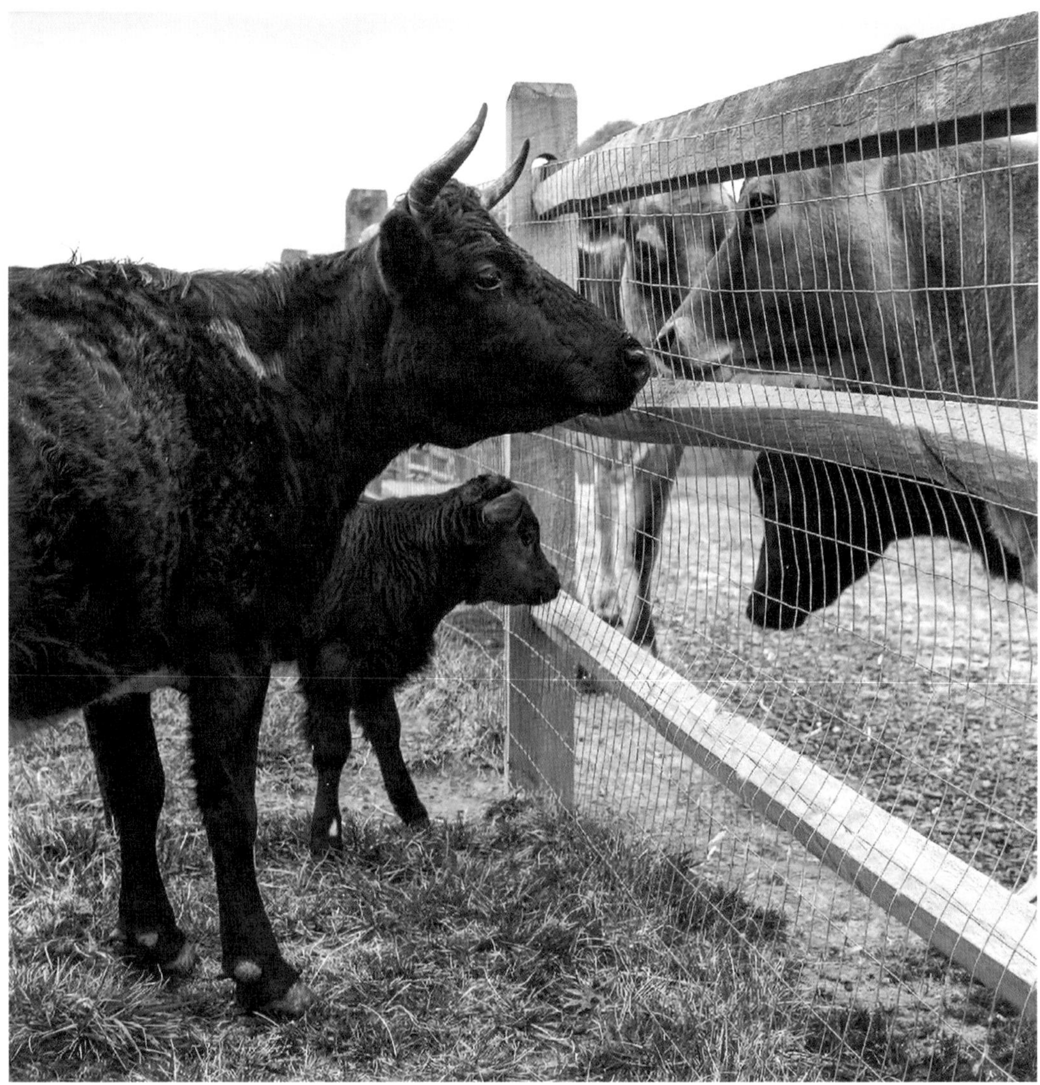

Cows in the herd greet new arrivals Ruby and Lucas (left) through the fence. Cows generally become very excited to meet new members of their herd. In turn, newly rescued cows in temporary quarantine have been known to break down fences or barn doors to meet their new herd.

Sanctuaries are sacred spaces. For animals rescued from traumatic circumstances, the road to healing can be long; but the people who run the sanctuaries work with the dispirited animal, offering physical nourishment and medical care, and encouraging words (and cookies) and as much distance as the animal needs to gradually gain trust.

Gaze long enough at the formerly farmed animals in a sanctuary, and they will gaze back. In their eyes you can see a residual reflection of mercy and kindness withheld. We recognize a shared spirit that yearns for acknowledgment and respect. Sanctuary is not just about rescuing animals, although that is the immediate mission. It's also about changing people's hearts—challenging us to live up to our stated morals—with the ultimate aim of reducing and someday eliminating the practices that make sanctuaries necessary in the first place.

Animal rights activists are often accused of attributing human characteristics to nonhuman animal behaviors. Love and joy, sadness and grief—these are beyond their cognitive and emotional capacities, the argument goes. But for too long, we shrugged off their natures as mere "instinct," genetic hardwiring, reducing them to machines. In recent decades, the results of serious scientific studies hint at the rich internal worlds of animals, familiar to any family with a beloved dog or cat.[8] While their expressions may differ from ours, the capacity of our fellow earthlings to feel and express complex motivations and social connections is undeniable.

Grief and mourning are not limited to primates such as humans and apes. Many animals exhibit behaviors that suggest they experience grief when a companion dies. These behaviors imply a level of emotional attachment and awareness of loss like what we humans experience. Cows have been known to approach the body of a beloved mate, smell and lick them, sometimes push their noses under the side or back end and attempt to help their friend to their feet. Failed attempts to essentially raise the dead result in low or loud cries and bellowing. Some cows have been observed holding vigil for hours or days over a burial site.[9]

The more we learn about the natures and needs of nonhumans, the more we notice how we are failing to meet our obligations to them. From industrialized animal agriculture and frenzied slaughterhouses to habitat loss and hunting operations, as well as antiquated and cruel experiments performed on animals in the name of science—we have fallen short in our duties to our fellow creatures.

Furthermore, factory farms are often located in marginalized communities. The manure lagoons, used to store animal waste, can leak contaminants into water supplies, and the air can be thick with ammonia and other harmful chemicals. These environmental hazards can lead to respiratory problems, asthma, and other health issues for residents.

Jobs in animal agriculture are often low-paying and have high rates of injury and illness. People of color are more likely to be employed in these jobs, putting them at greater risk.

As consumers, we're empowered to make a meaningful difference when we shop. To take the most obvious example, the demand for healthier alternatives to meat, dairy, and eggs has given rise in recent years to oat, cashew, and a plethora of other milk options as well as a wide range of plant-based burgers and chicken, cheese, and egg substitutes that can satisfy our appetites. The choices you and I make can both taste good and have a profound impact on the lives of animals.

In the pages of this book, I invite you to see members of a herd as individuals—drifting across peaceful pastures like clouds, mingling and clustering together. A mother pours her love into the child she was serendipitously allowed to keep; a particular cow presses the side of his head against the strong, solid expanse of his best friend's withers and girth. Each one expresses their own disposition, as intricate and varied as a spider's web in the morning dew. And yet, these rescued cows are only special insofar as they are among the lucky few to have been freed from systems and practices that devalue them.

Let's amble alongside the cows awhile and celebrate not only their moral dignity but also their resilient and sensitive natures. Thank you for sharing this journey with me.

For a kinder world.

SANCTUARIES REPRESENTED IN THIS BOOK

Chenoa Manor

733 Glen Willow Rd
Avondale, PA 19311
https://www.chenoamanor.org/
Facebook: @chenoamanor
Instagram: @chenoamanor
X: @chenoamanorfarm

Critter Creek Farm Sanctuary

12626 NW Co Rd 231
Gainesville, FL 32609
https://crittercreekfarmsanctuary.org/
Facebook: @crittercreekfarmsanctuary
Instagram: @crittercreekfarmsanctuary
TikTok: @crittercreekfs
X: @Critter_Creek

Indraloka Animal Sanctuary

336 Oak Dr
Dalton, PA 18414
(570) 763-2908
https://indraloka.org/
Facebook: @IndralokaAS
Instagram: @indralokasanctuary
X: @IndralokaAS

Lancaster Farm Sanctuary

1871 Milton Grove Rd
Mount Joy, PA 17552
https://lancasterfarmsanctuary.org/
Facebook: @lancasterfarmsanctuary
Instagram: @lancasterfarmsanctuary

Luvin Arms Animal Sanctuary

3470 Co Rd 7
Erie, CO 80516
https://luvinarms.org/
Facebook: @luvinarms
Instagram: @luvinarms

Peaceful Fields Sanctuary

153 Peacefield Ln
Winchester, VA 22603
https://peacefulfieldssanctuary.org/
Facebook: @peacefulfieldssanctuary
Instagram: @peacefulfieldssanctuary
X: @PFsanctuary

Poplar Spring Animal Sanctuary

15200 Mount Nebo Rd
Poolesville, MD 20837
(301) 428-8128
https://www.animalsanctuary.org/
Facebook: @PoplarSpringAnimal
Instagram: @poplarspringsanctuary

Rosie's Farm Sanctuary

10717 Tulip Ln
Potomac, MD 20854
https://rosiesfarmsanctuary.org/
Facebook: @rosiesfarmsanctuary
Instagram: @rosiesfarmsanctuary
X: @RosiesFS

Safe Haven Farm Sanctuary

254 Gardner Hollow Rd
Poughquag, NY 12570
(845) 724-5138
https://safehavenfarmsanctuary.org/
Facebook: @safehavenfarmsanctuary
Instagram: @safehavenfarmsanctuary

Star Gazing Farm Animal Sanctuary

16760 Whites Store Rd
Boyds, MD 20841
(301) 674-5716
https://www.stargazingfarm.org/
Facebook: @stargazingfarmanimalsanctuary
Instagram: @stargazingfarmanimalsanctuary

COW PORTRAITS AND SANCTUARY STORIES

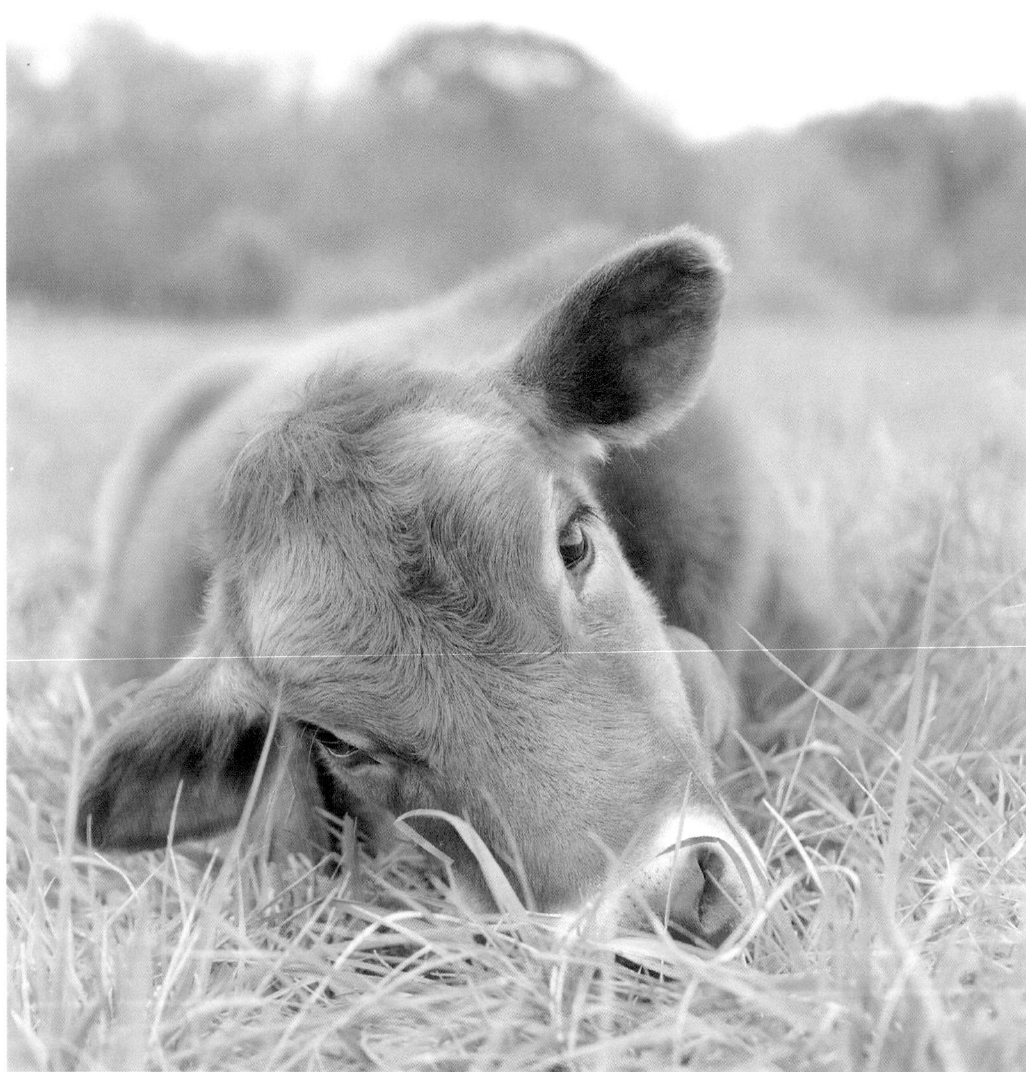

Juliet *(Jersey)*

Juliet was rescued with her friend Clifford from a backyard farm, where they were shackled to a tree with heavy chains and had no shelter from the weather. Neighbors saw them in distress during storms, tangled in their chains and unable to move. When confronted, the farmer threatened to kill the cows. An animal control officer convinced the owner to instead give up custody of the calves.

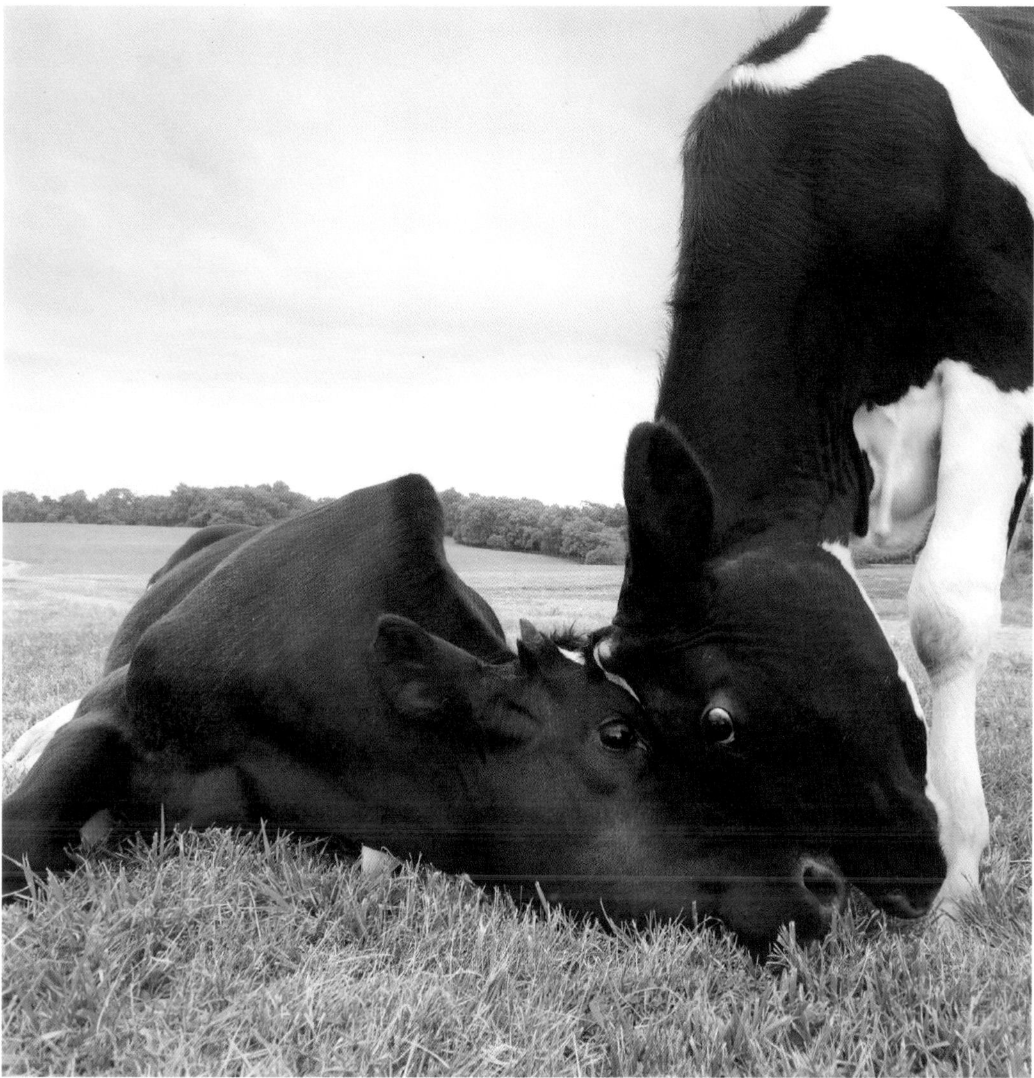

Mikey *(Holstein) and* ***Clifford*** *(Holstein)*

A roadside produce stand had a petting zoo. At the end of the growing season, Mikey was to be slaughtered. In a twist of fate, Mikey injured his back. The employee who nursed him back to health felt compassion and purchased him to save his life.

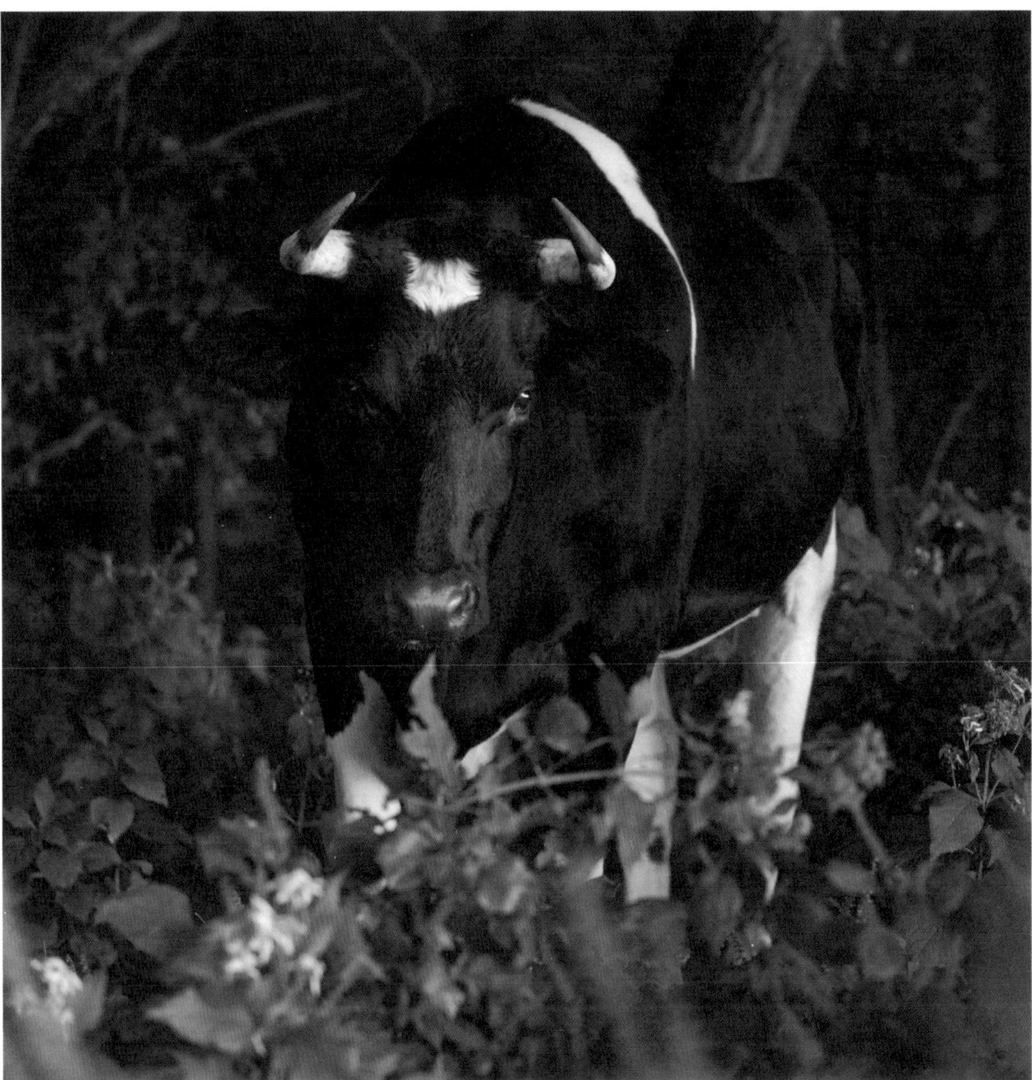

Moses *(Holstein)*

Moses was born on an Amish dairy farm. When the veal truck came to collect the male calves, his mother hid him, having likely lost many calves before and wanting to protect him. The farmer, furious to find Moses after the truck left, separated him from his mother and left him to starve. A woman who was visiting convinced the farmer to let her take Moses to a sanctuary.

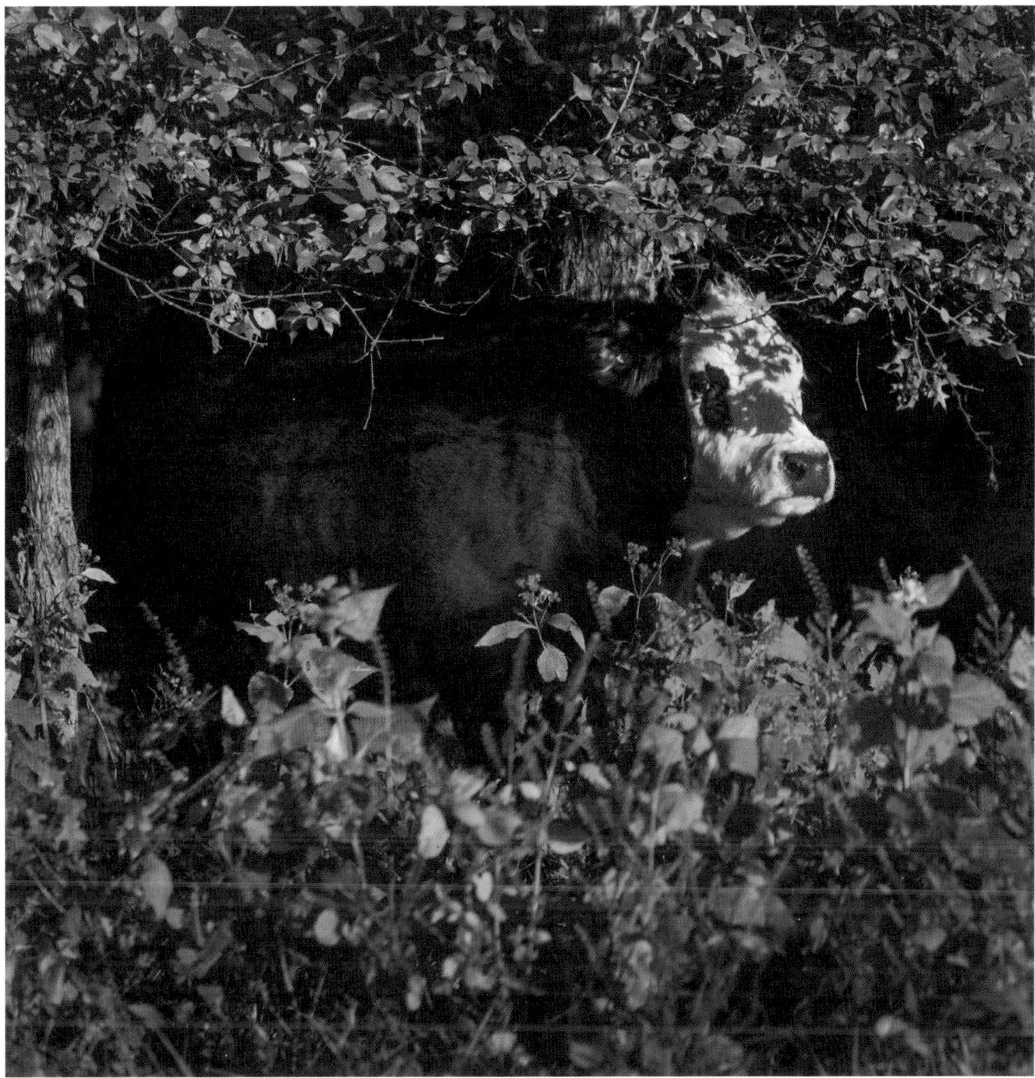

Wallace *(Hereford/Angus cross)*

On the long drive to a livestock auction, the gate of a transport truck broke, and Wallace tumbled onto the highway. Injured, he jumped a guard rail and ran into the woods, where he survived for two weeks as authorities tried to capture him. When his legal owner told police to "just shoot him," a sanctuary stepped in, hiring local cowboys to rescue him before delivering him to his permanent home.

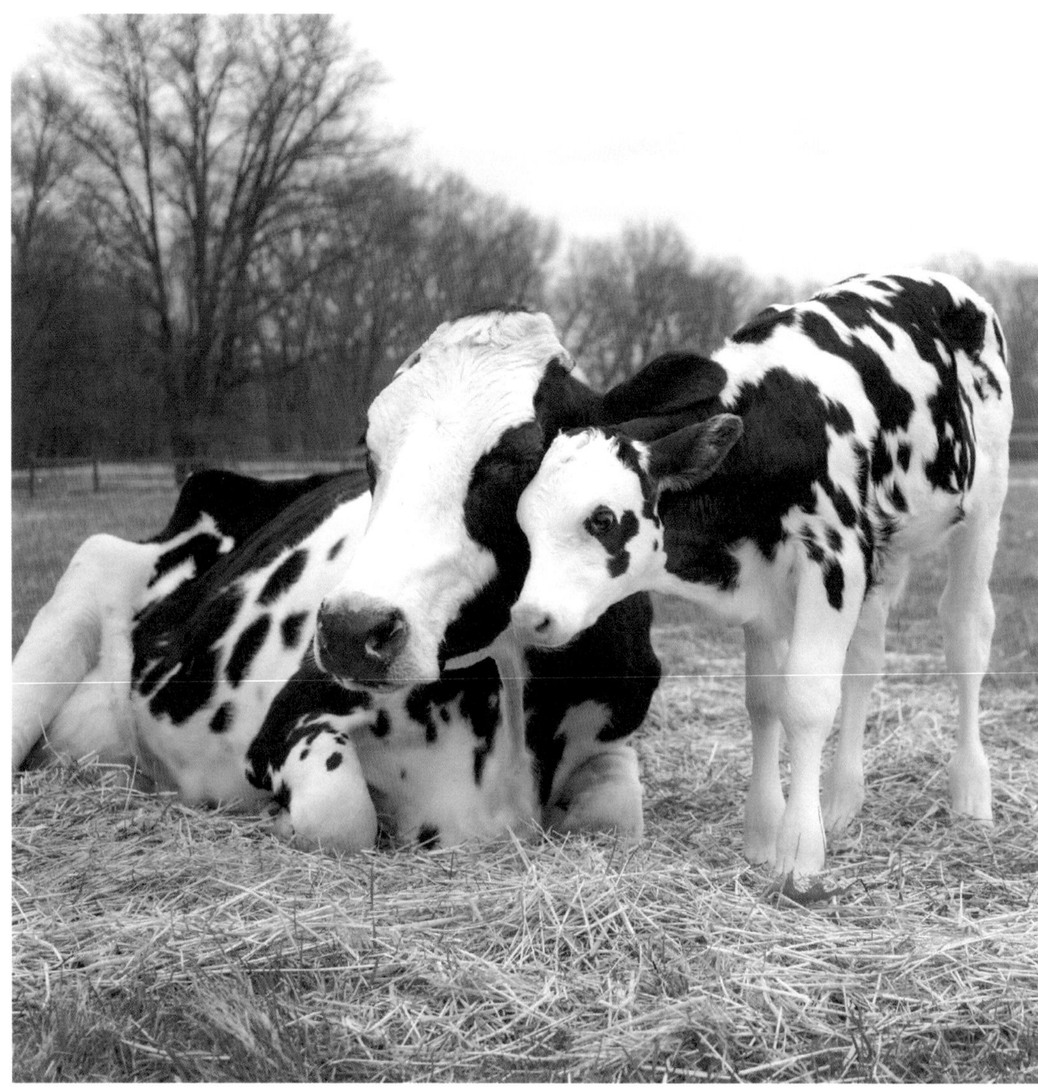

Maisie *(Holstein) and* ***Justin*** *(Holstein)*

Photographed in 2018. When Maisie was young, she occasionally leaped over her fence on a small dairy farm to play with the farmer's dogs. She followed people around the farm and enjoyed receiving attention. When the dairy farm closed, Maisie arrived in a sanctuary pregnant with Justin.

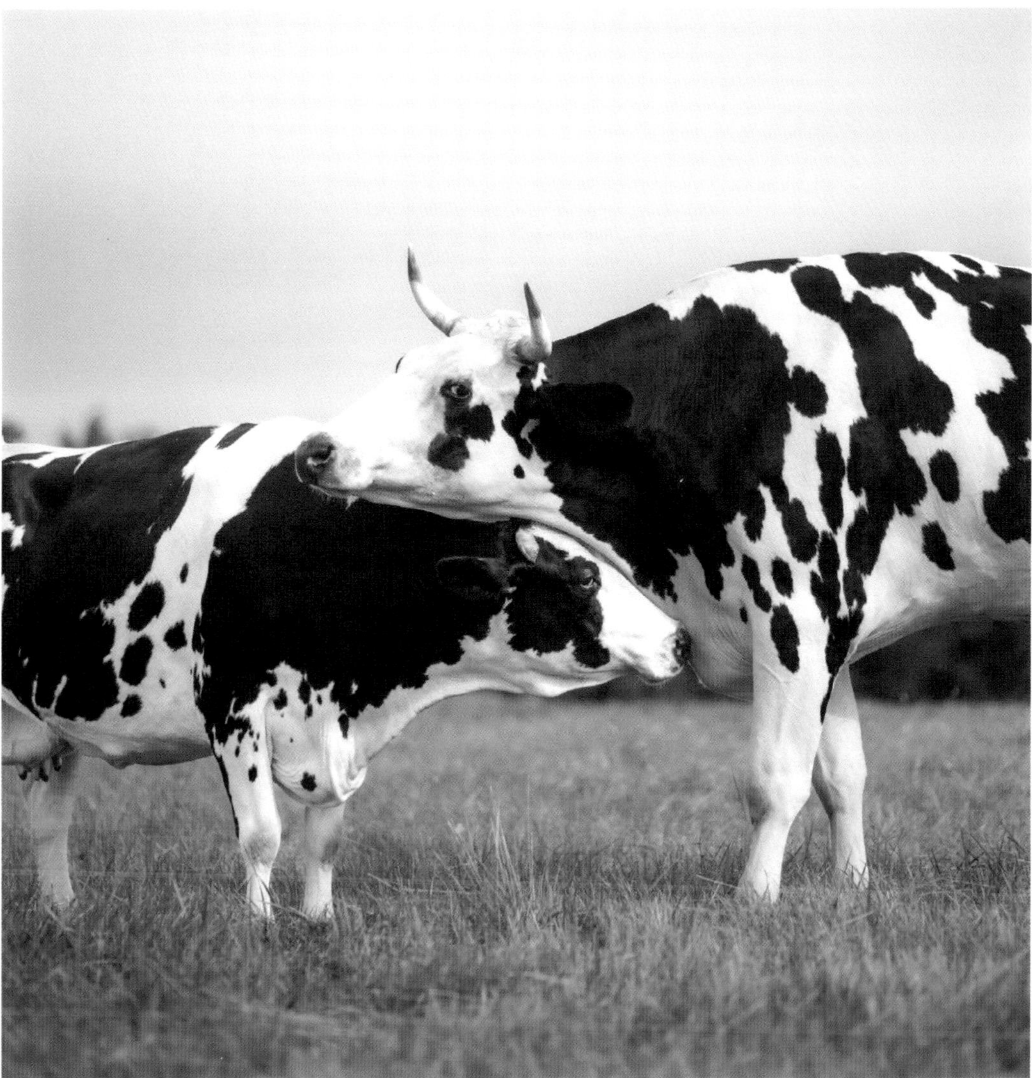

Maisie *and* ***Justin***

Photographed in 2023. Maisie and Justin have lived together in a herd for over six years, and their relationship is as close as ever. Throughout each day, Maisie still grooms Justin for long periods of time, even when it starts to annoy him. "Oh, Mom!," you could imagine him saying. But he is the only one of her children she was allowed to raise. They lie beside each other and touch each other frequently.

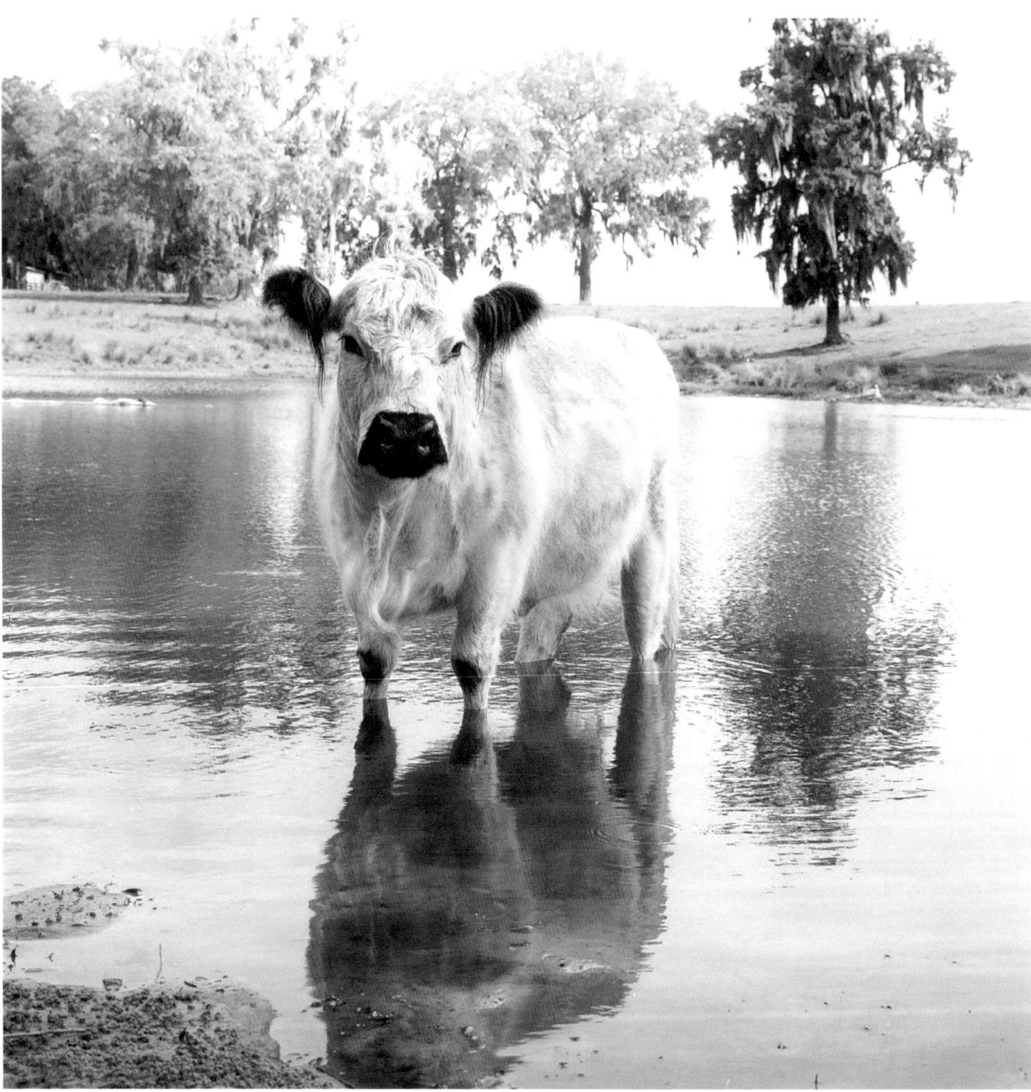

Pepper *(British White)*

Pepper lived with her best friend, Seymour, a water buffalo rescued from the dairy industry. While their legal owner treated Seymour as a pet, he bred Pepper repeatedly to produce calves for slaughter. When the owner's mother decided to sell the property they lived on, he chose to find Seymour a home. He requested that whoever took Seymour also take Pepper and Truffles, her final calf, to keep their little family together.

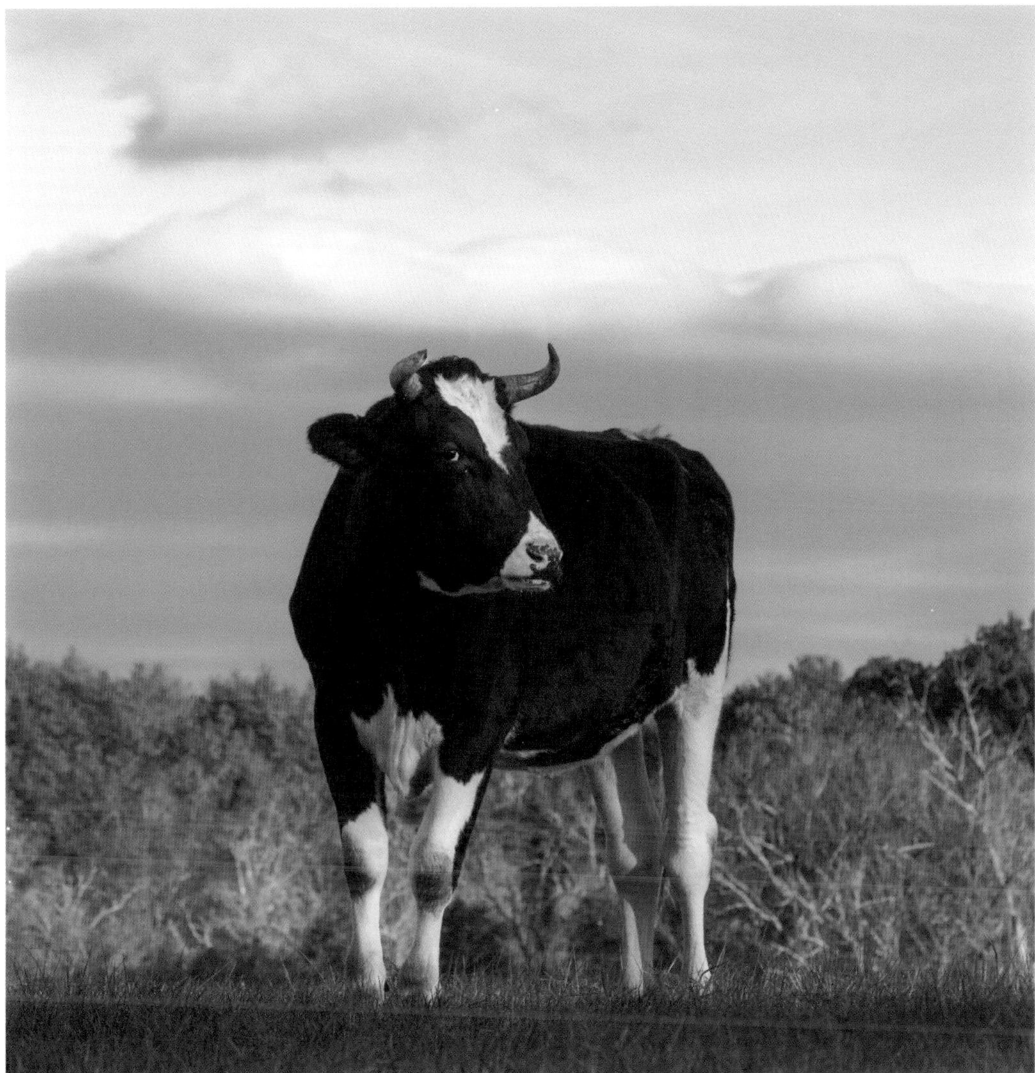

Edison *(Holstein)*

Edison and his best friend, Eddie, were rescued from a farm where they were starving, with a Body Condition Score of 1.5 out of 5. They suffered from urine scalding and hair loss from lying in their waste. Despite farmed animals being exempt from most anti-cruelty laws, the farm owner was found legally guilty of cruelty and ordered to provide restitution for their care.

STAR GAZING FARM ANIMAL SANCTUARY

Anne Shroeder, Founder
Boyds, Maryland

Sweet Carmen

(Photograph on page 82)

Sweet, railroad boxcar–shaped, fuzzy, blind girl with unerring navigational radar—Carmen has not often taken center stage. Well, it's about time!

Carmen, when asked, has noted that it's very tiresome that the naughty ones—Petey, who walks through fences like they are made of toothpicks, and young Wilbur, who bucks and rears and thinks every human is his personal toy—steal the show. But isn't that always the way; those who make trouble garner the headlines, causing people to squeak or jump fences or curse at the seemingly never-ending destruction. "Oh, Petey!" they cry out in frustration and affection.

Yet those who go about their peaceful days grazing, exploring the fields and the shade trees, sitting quietly with the sheep, those whose very existence is a blessing and a balm—they are often seen only out of the corner of the eye. It seems very unfair.

Carmen came to Star Gazing Farm at four months of age. She had suffered a terrible illness when she was little that had rendered her blind. Her ultimate destination was supposed to be the auction, but the farmer, having nursed her out of sepsis and seen her recover, could not bear to load her, blind and confused, onto the trailer bound for an unhappy end.

This kind of cognitive dissonance is not uncommon.

When Carmen first arrived, we led her into a stall with a small adjoining paddock. It is our quarantine area, where we bring new animals to the farm both for medical observation and to allow them to adjust psychologically to their new surroundings. She immediately started going around and around and around in circles. We tried to stop her. We could not stop her. We thought, "She's going to get dizzy." We wondered, "Does she have a neurological condition?" We fretted quite a lot. But around and around she went. And then she stopped. She had confirmed and reconfirmed the boundaries of her new home. When she was slowly introduced to other areas of the farm, she seemed to know just where the fences were. She avoided the trucks and tractor and found her way quite easily to the hay bales and water troughs.

We surmised that, very likely, she could see shadows, so accurately did she navigate our hilly farm. A few months after we first adopted her, we took her up to the University of Pennsylvania veterinary hospital to see an ophthalmologist. Her eyes protruded and rolled around a little bit, and so a visit to the doctor seemed wise. The diagnosis: healthy, but 100% blind. What a remarkable little-big cow.

Carmen, unlike our other cows Petey and Wilbur, was lucky to have grown up with her mama. She had suffered an almost fatal illness, but nevertheless had the love and licks of her big Hereford mama. And she passed that on. A year after her arrival, Carmen helped raise a special-needs lamb. Every photo of little Ricardo included Carmen. Ricardo claimed the limelight while Carmen was simply there. Warm, copper-colored, fuzzy Carmen was there for all who needed her. But being there is more than a lot of people accomplish in a whole lifetime.

> "A friend is someone who helps you up when you're down, and if they can't, they lay down beside you and listen."—Winnie the Pooh

Carmen also took on the mothering of Wilbur. Wilbur's mother, Rosie, died shortly after giving birth to him. Five days later, some dogs attacked him, inflicting a serious wound on his knee joint. He came to us shortly thereafter, and we quickly transported him to the hospital. Upon his return, Carmen would stand by him and lick his face. His poor mother had also been a piebald Hereford, like Carmen. Healing for animals can sometimes take a surprising path. It would be wise to never underestimate any creature—four-legged, two-legged, or winged.

One time, I was out in the pasture doing some cleanup. I reached down to pick something up, and Carmen came around right behind me, head butted me squarely center on my bum, and knocked me over. I was incredibly impressed at her aim. I think she was quite pleased with herself, not ordinarily indulging in hijinks.

Aside from the head butt she issued me only once, Carmen has shown only gentleness toward our volunteers, visitors, and, of course, the other animals. You can sit down on the ground with her and groom her and pet her and she just soaks up the love. There is a kind of peace when you lean against a cow that is very hard to describe. They are solid. They are grounded. They are massive. They are warm and hairy. I really can't think of anything better.

Is good press important? What about bad press? Is any attention worth it? Our boys think so. Whenever we have visitors, Petey, our enormous Brown Swiss steer, bounds up to the fence, insisting on giving hard sandpaper licks to the visitors, charming them, showing off his large fuzzy ears and generally overshadowing everyone else on the farm because, "Oh my gosh, he's so huge! Oh my gosh, I've never seen an animal this big! He's so cute! Look at this enormous cow, isn't he wonderful?" Of course, they were never squashed by him against a fence when he decided it was time to play, nor chased by him through the field when he thought we had something in our hands he might want. Petey is a terror, and Wilbur is fast following in his footsteps.

Carmen, sweet Carmen, has always quietly gone about her business, navigating a completely dark world where the only light she can feel is the sunshine on her beautiful brown back. Carmen is kind and patient. It's so easy to talk and write about the ones who are naughty. Who are dramatic. Who burst into the house or get into people's cars or have tremendous recovery from awful wounds. Carmen did have a miraculous recovery before she got here. That was her drama, and that was enough for one lifetime for a little cow.

Now it is time to simply be here.

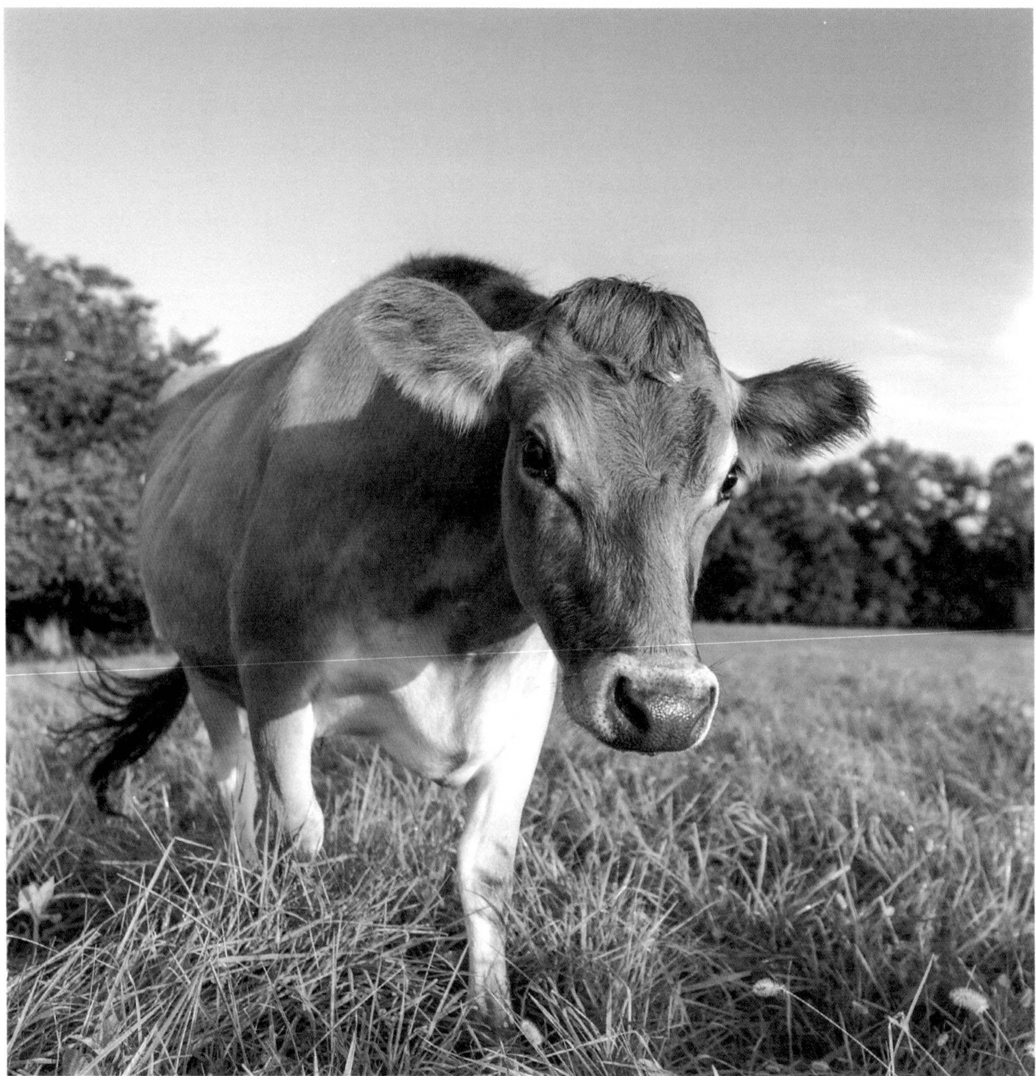

Jessie *(Jersey)*

While Jessie's mother was pregnant with him, her legal owner fed her so little she was emaciated, with ribs and backbone showing. An animal protection group confiscated her, provided care, and filed charges against the owner. The case took a year to resolve with appeals, during which Jessie was born. When the case was resolved, a kind person adopted Jessie's mother, and Jessie was given a home in a sanctuary.

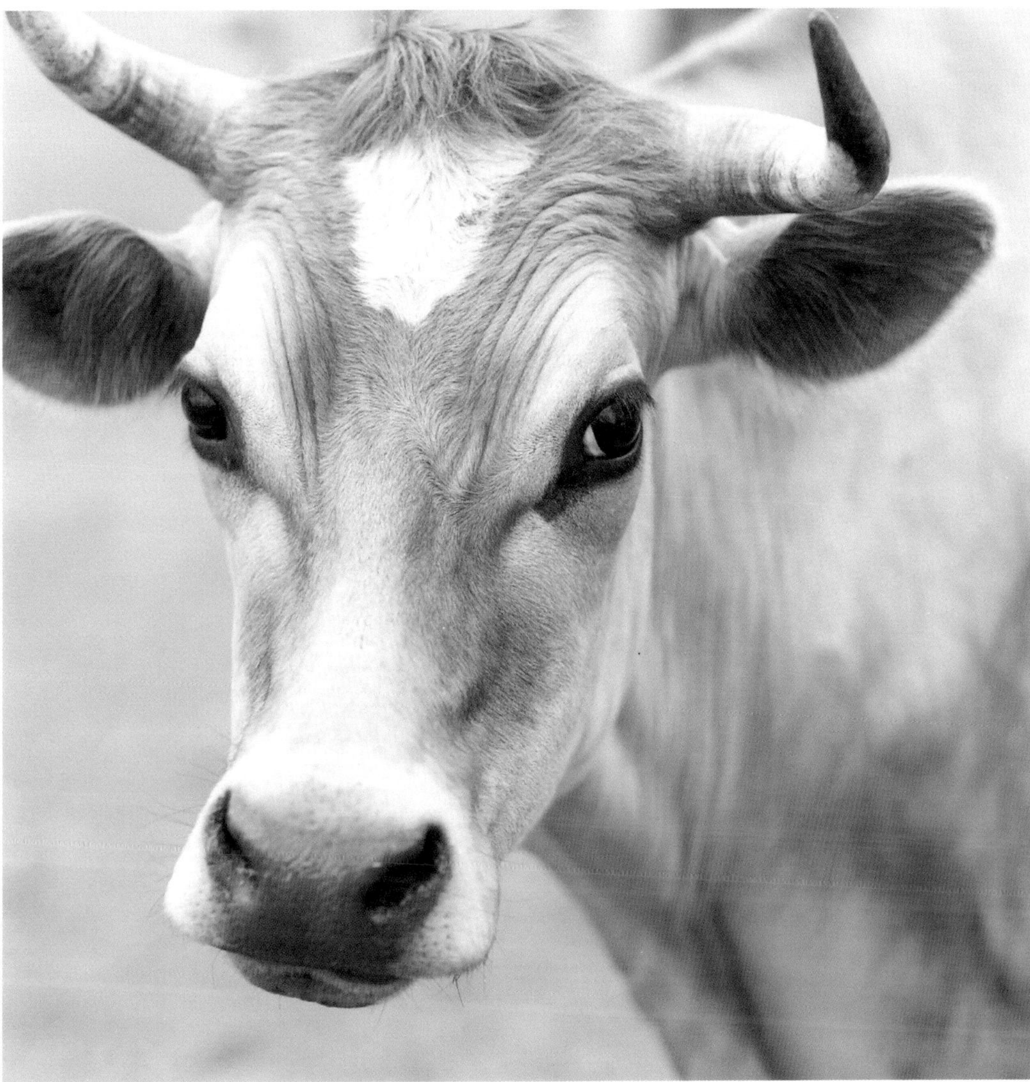

Bolero *(Jersey)*

Bolero was born on a dairy farm and purchased as a calf to save him from being slaughtered. When he outgrew his caretaker's resources, a permanent home was found for him in a sanctuary.

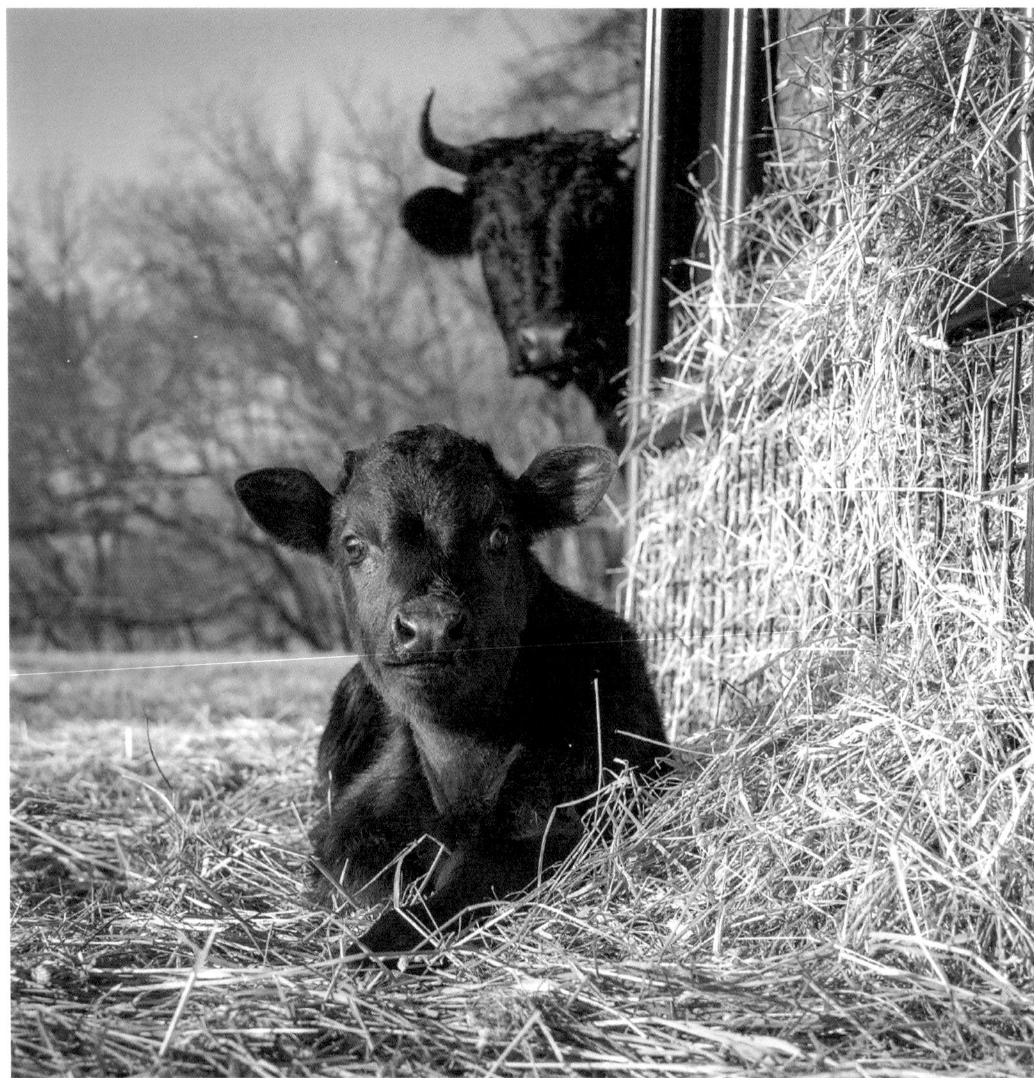

***Ruby** (Dexter) and **Lucas** (Dexter)*

Ruby gave birth to Lucas in a kill pen at a livestock auction. Kill pens hold farmed animals in cramped conditions until they are auctioned for slaughter. A horse rescuer noticed Ruby with tears in her eyes and couldn't forget her. She decided to rescue Ruby and her fragile baby. They were delivered to an animal hospital, where Lucas almost died. After he regained his health, they were taken to a sanctuary.

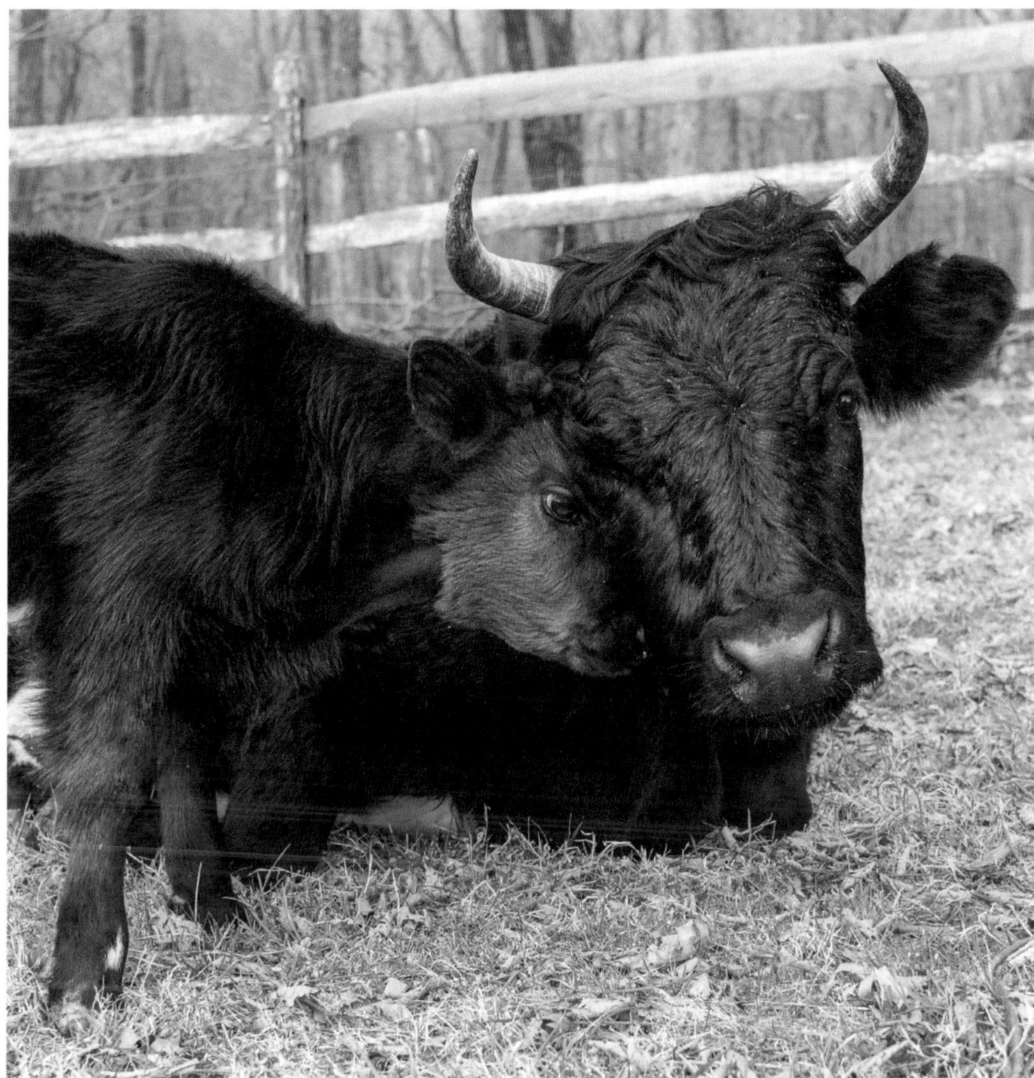

Ruby *and* ***Lucas***

Lucas snuggles in the warmth of his mother's accommodating body. Close physical contact helps to strengthen the bond between the mother and calf and provides the calf with a sense of security. In sanctuary settings, you can often see mother cows lying down next to their calves, gently touching them with their heads or bodies, which is one way they express care and affection.

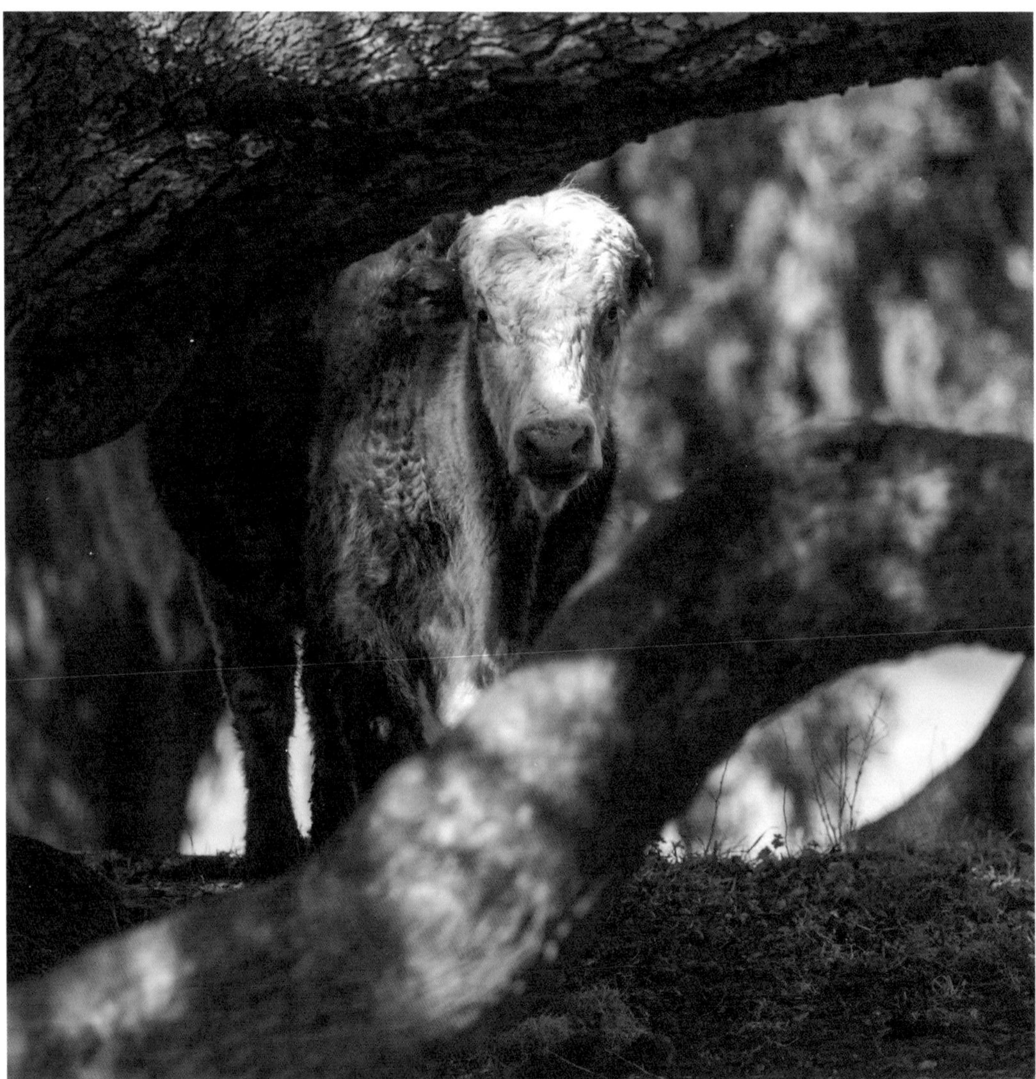

Vincent van Moo *(Hereford)*

Vincent van Moo was rescued by the South Florida SPCA after he was mauled by dogs. The dogs tore off one of his ears entirely, and the other one was shredded. After surgery and a lot of tender-loving care, he has made a full recovery.

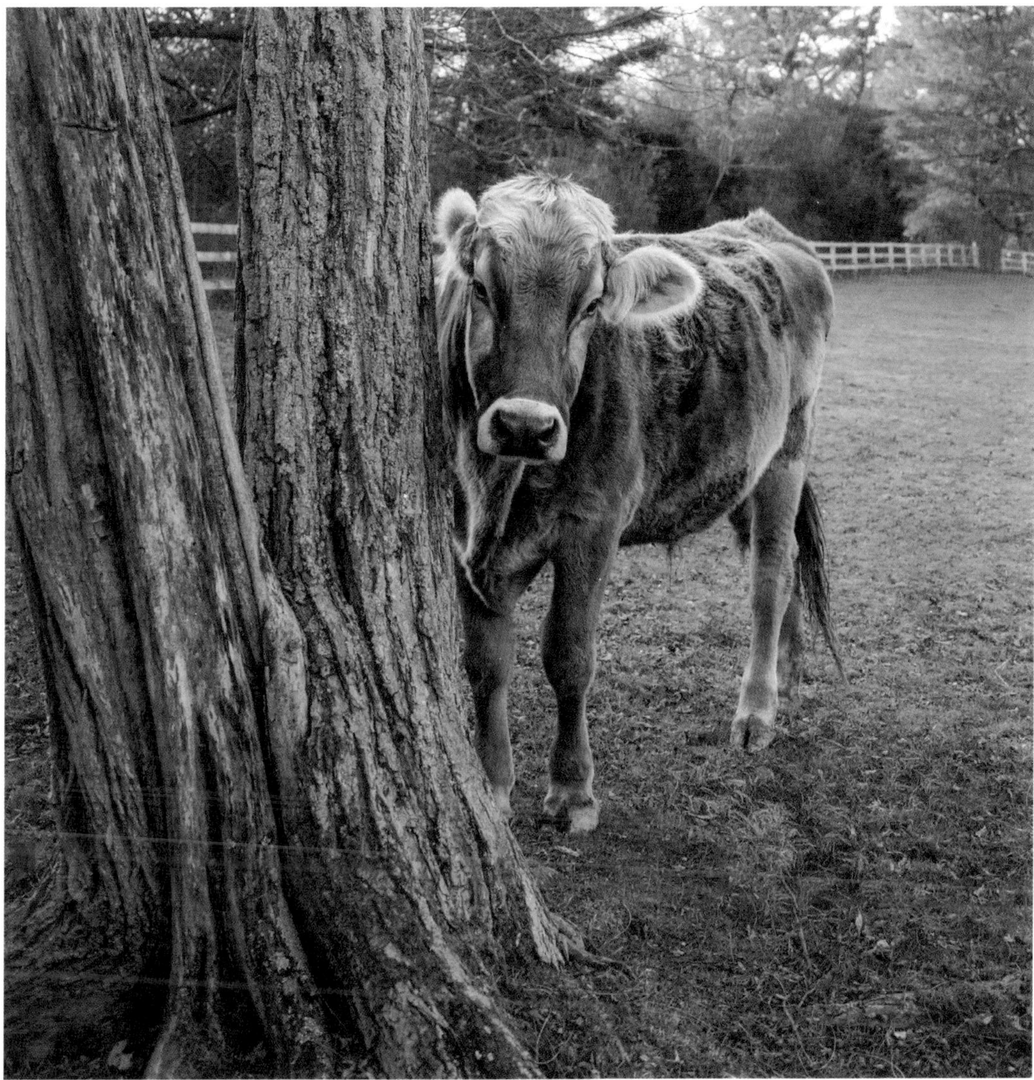

Petey *(Brown Swiss)*

Born on a dairy farm where male calves are raised for meat, Petey was rejected by his mother and left in a muddy field. A kind worker rescued him, giving him a second chance. At the sanctuary, he eagerly greets visitors, inviting strokes on his soft brown head and offering sandpapery kisses. Those who enter his pasture sometimes meet a playful, joyful steer, leaping and racing to and fro. As he grows, Petey will likely settle down—realizing his 2,000-pound frame gives him an unfair advantage in his favorite games.

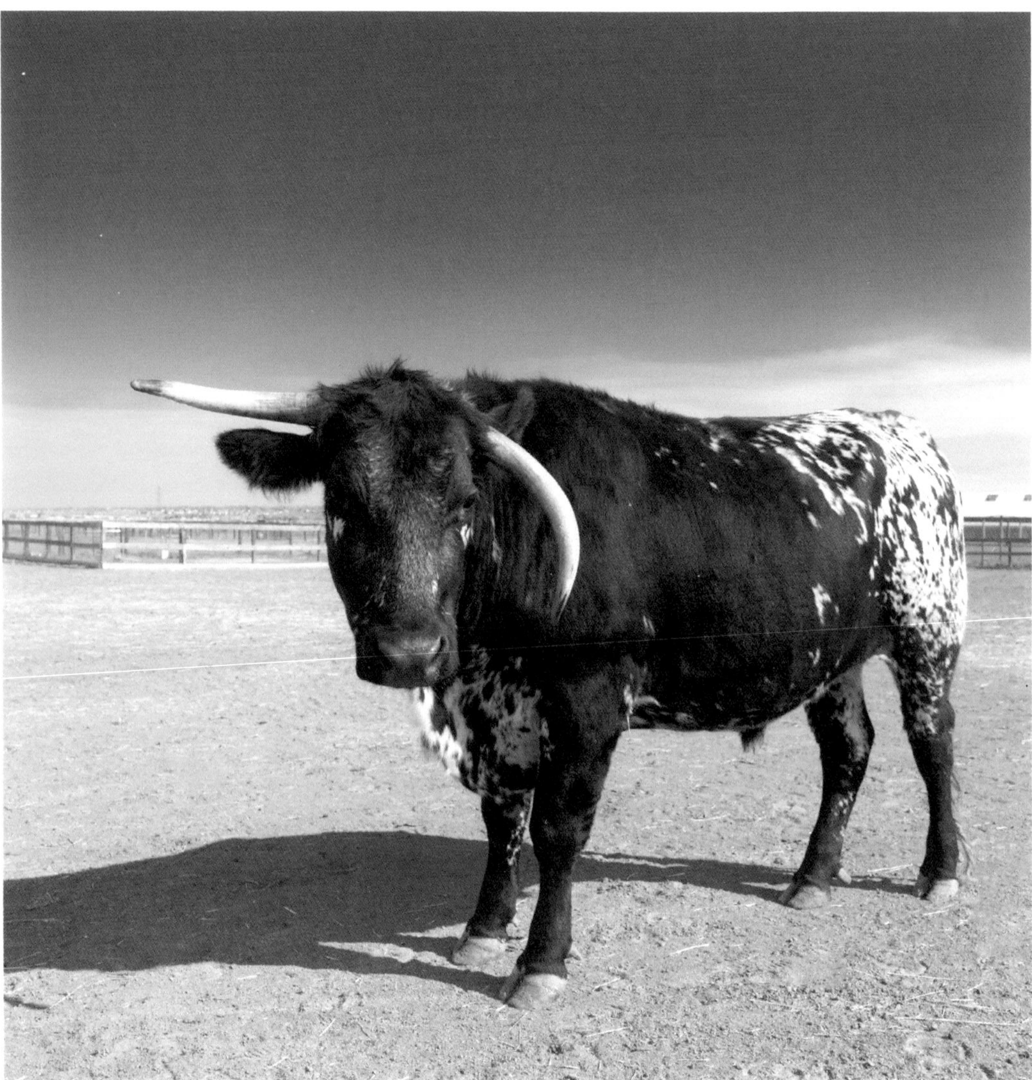

Lucky *(Speckle Park)*

Lucky enjoys chasing the care team at the sanctuary, who ride around the cow pasture in buggies with treats such as timothy hay or crunchy leaves to dispense. *See "Lucky" on page 35.*

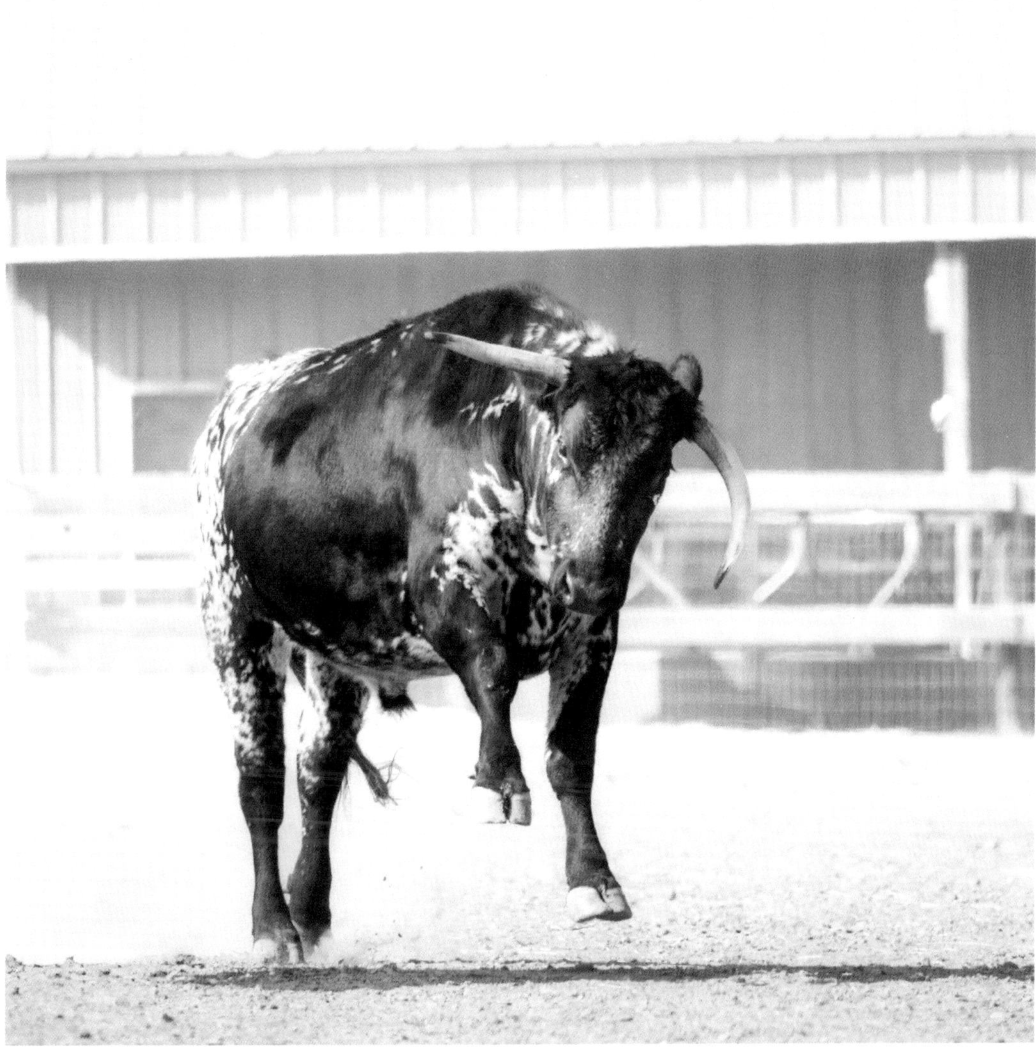

Lucky

Lucky and his cow friends receive enrichment in the form of "treat tubes" of special hay; and as someone who loves treats, he gets very excited. They are also learning to be "clicker trained," a positive-reinforcement method similar to dog training. This training is not only fun and enriching but also promotes cooperative care.

LUVIN ARMS ANIMAL SANCTUARY

Kelly Nix, Managing Director
Erie, Colorado

Lucky

(Photographs on pages 32 and 33)

At Luvin Arms Animal Sanctuary, we've had the privilege of witnessing and being a part of many heartwarming stories. Still, few have touched us quite like the tale of Lucky, a cow whose life journey epitomizes the essence of resilience, love, and the profound connections that transcend species.

Lucky's mother was raised to be slaughtered for meat on a ranch in Arizona. While pregnant with Lucky, wolves attacked and killed her. Miraculously, her calf was pulled from her and survived—the first lucky break in his life. Initially cared for by the ranching family's children, Lucky was brought into their home, fed, and treated as a pet. Yet, beneath this seemingly fortunate beginning lay a grim reality: Lucky was still being raised for slaughter.

When Lucky grew to near slaughter size, he was transported to a property in Lyons, Colorado, to be killed. As fate would have it, his pasture was adjacent to a pleasant road popular with walkers. On a serene morning, a schoolteacher on a walk spotted Lucky. Their eyes met across the fence, and a remarkable bond was forged. Lucky followed her along the fence, responding to her words and showing a yearning for connection that moved her. That same day, she brought her husband to meet her cow friend.

This bond between the couple and Lucky grew with daily visits over a period of months. Lucky was profoundly lonely; he craved human affection and companionship. He greeted his friends eagerly when they visited him, indulging in playful activities and brushing sessions that provided him with much needed love and attention. They often stayed for hours and gave him nose scratches and even hugs over the fence. To their surprise, the couple learned that many other members of the local community had discovered and befriended Lucky.

Lucky's friends learned that he was destined to be slaughtered for meat. The news was a devastating blow to those who had grown to love him. Some struggled internally, conflicted about the destiny of farm animals like him; however, the pain of losing Lucky spurred them into action.

The first critical step was finding Lucky a safe haven, which led them to us at Luvin Arms. We were contacted and, understanding the urgency of Lucky's situation, agreed to provide him with a forever home.

Next came the challenge of convincing his legal owner to release Lucky. The couple rallied the community, who helped secure Lucky's freedom.

Lucky was finally brought to Luvin Arms! His arrival at the sanctuary was a moment of celebration and hope. His need for emotional and physical connection was palpable, and he quickly became a cherished member of our Luvin Arms family. One of the "big boys" in the herd, Tito, had recently lost his close friend and had been visibly mourning for months. To integrate Lucky into his new herd safely, we placed him in a temporary holding area where the cows could all meet each other over a fence. Well! Tito would have none of that. He seemed to recognize Lucky as a kindred spirit. Tito broke the fence in his enthusiasm to reach his new friend. Their bond continues to this day.

Lucky's story at Luvin Arms has not been without challenges. His previous diet, standard in the beef industry to fatten cows quickly for slaughter, left him with digestive issues. Our dedicated team has worked tirelessly to rehabilitate his health, ensuring he enjoys the fullest life possible.

Today, Lucky's story stands as a powerful testament to the complex emotional lives of farmed animals and the transformative power of compassion. It underscores our mission at Luvin Arms: to provide sanctuary and advocate for beings often misunderstood and neglected. Lucky's journey from a doomed fate to a life filled with love and care continues to inspire us and our community, reminding us of the profound connections possible when we choose love and kindness over indifference.

Samantha

(Photograph on pages 105)

Born on a neighboring dairy farm, Samantha's fate was seemingly sealed from the moment of her birth. In industry terms, Samantha was born a *freemartin*. A freemartin is defined as a heifer (female) that is born a twin with a bull (male) and is most always sterile as a result of shared male and female hormones in the mother's uterus. Exposure to male hormones leads to underdevelopment of the female's reproductive tract. This anomaly meant that Samantha most likely could not be impregnated. In a world where productivity dictates value, she was therefore worthless to the dairy operation. She likely would have been sent to a livestock auction and sold to be butchered for cheap meat. Instead, the management of the dairy farm agreed to relinquish the calf to Luvin Arms Animal Sanctuary.

Upon her arrival, Samantha was visibly shaken and nervous around humans. However, the new girl was about to make a best friend.

Marley Rose, only nine days older than Samantha, was also born a freemartin on a dairy farm. Rescued shortly before Samantha arrived, Marley Rose was kept separate from the boys in the cow herd, who were much larger than her. Although she had friends among the sheep, she clearly longed for companionship among her own kind. We put out the word among the local farms that we were looking for a female calf, and the dairy farm gave us Samantha rather than sending her to auction.

While Samantha was in quarantine—a short period during which a new arrival receives her vaccinations—you could hear Marley Rose and Samantha mooing back and forth to each other between the walls. Once she was cleared to join Marley Rose in the big barn, her new "big sister" helped teach her the language of ease and trust through their daily interactions—grazing and playing in pastures and cuddling during peaceful slumbers. Marley Rose frequently licked Samantha to calm her and show affection. Their bond, nurtured by the sanctuary staff's compassionate care, grew into a deep friendship. Once timid, Samantha grew curious and confident.

Samantha's story highlights the often-overlooked complexities of farmed animals' lives and challenges the acceptability of their treatment in industries that view them as mere commodities. Her life at Luvin Arms, enriched with genuine care and respect, is filled with the warmth of a community that values her not for her utility but for her inherent worth.

Today, Samantha thrives alongside her fellow sanctuary residents. Her journey from a disregarded byproduct of the dairy industry to a cherished individual exemplifies the core mission of Luvin Arms—to advocate for those who have not been rescued by sharing our residents' stories to inspire, educate, and empower others to embrace a more compassionate and sustainable lifestyle.

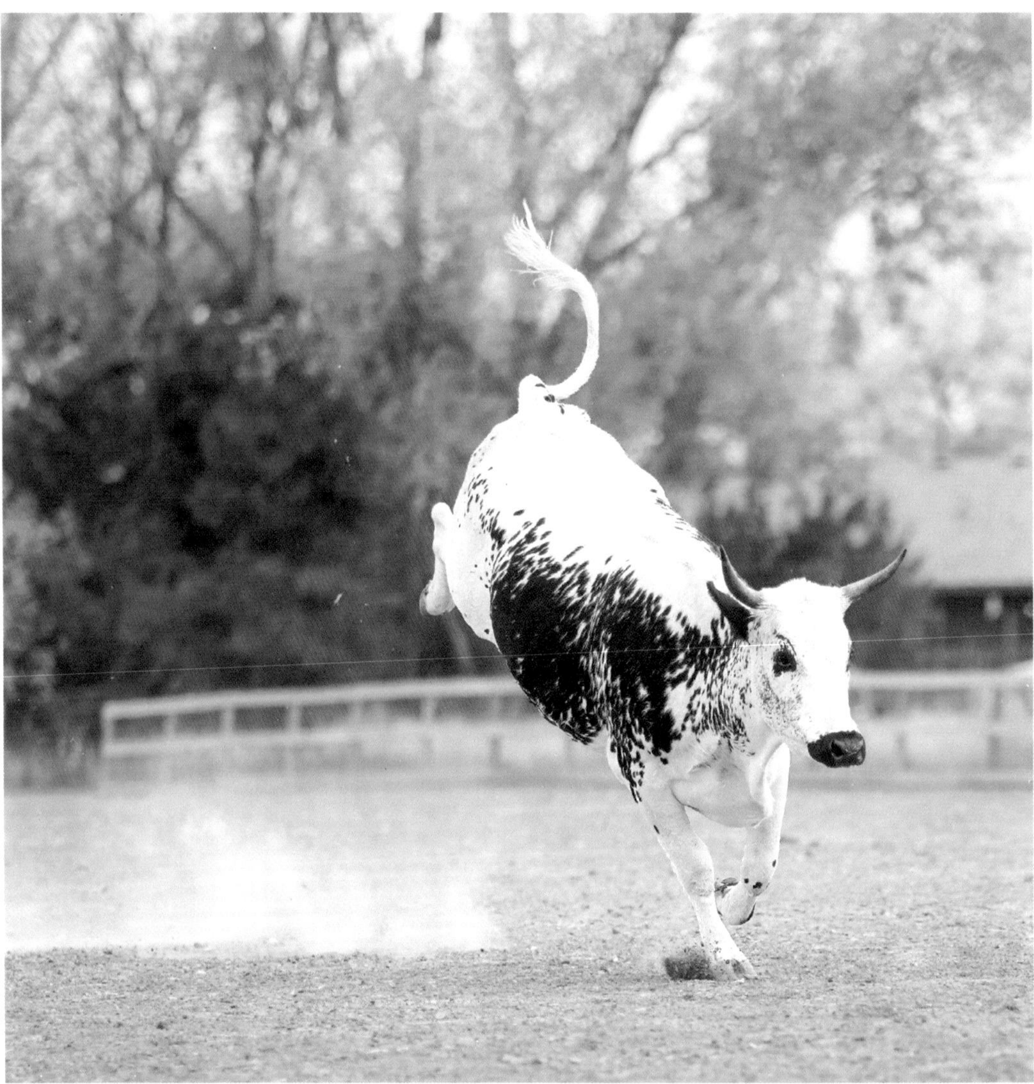

Laxmi *(Speckle Park/Holstein mix)*

A kind soul from the Colorado Jain Indian community rescued Laxmi's mother, Devi, from a dairy ranch, unaware she was pregnant. At under two years old, Devi was too young to be a mother, but she defied the odds, delivering Laxmi on the coldest day in Aurora, Colorado, in 77 years. Mother and daughter now live together.

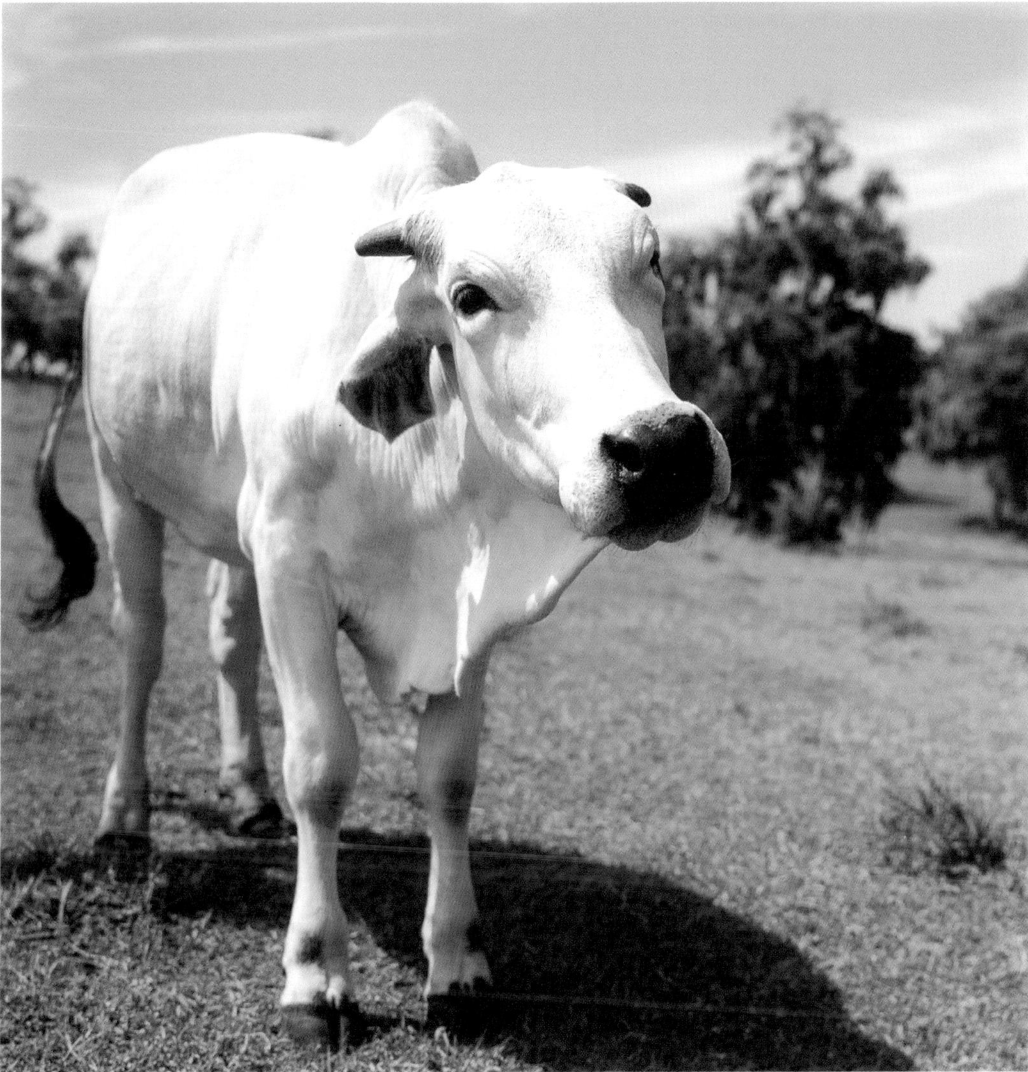

***Bentley** (Brahman)*

Bentley was born on a cattle ranch with "dummy calf" syndrome, a condition caused by a lack of oxygen at birth. Unable to nurse from his mother or a bottle, he was unprofitable for the farm. Fortunately, they surrendered Bentley to a local sanctuary. The staff struggled to get him to eat until they introduced him to Stanley, another cow who had overcome similar challenges. Stanley helped teach Bentley by example.

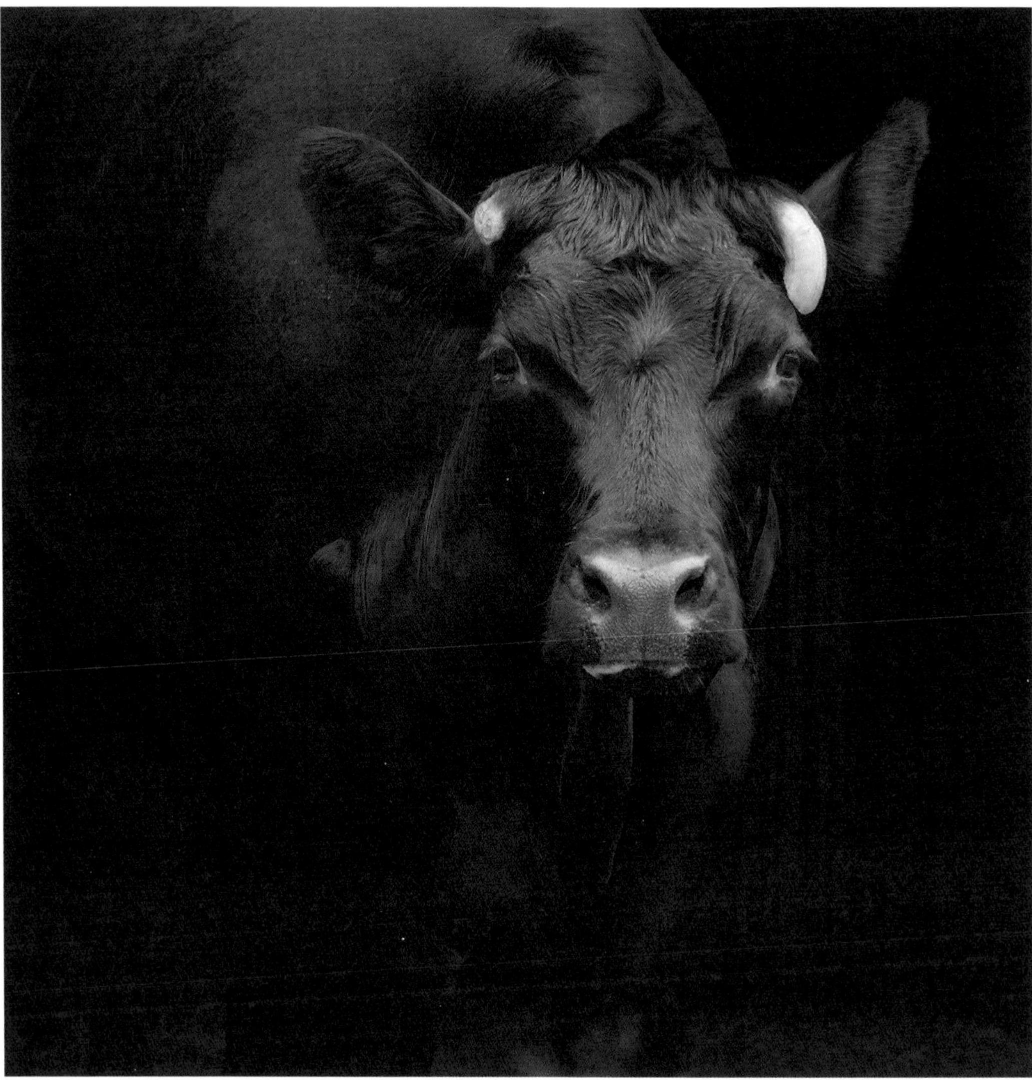

***Jason** (Angus)*

A double-decker tractor-trailer carrying Jason and 120 other cows to a feedlot in Kansas crashed near Pittsburgh, Pennsylvania, killing all but 30 on impact. Animals are often transported long distances to feedlots and slaughterhouses, enduring extreme heat, cold, thirst, and hunger.

While many breeds of cow raised for meat are naturally polled (hornless), calves with horn buds undergo disbudding, typically with a hot iron or caustic paste. Incomplete disbudding can result in partial horn growth, called scurs.

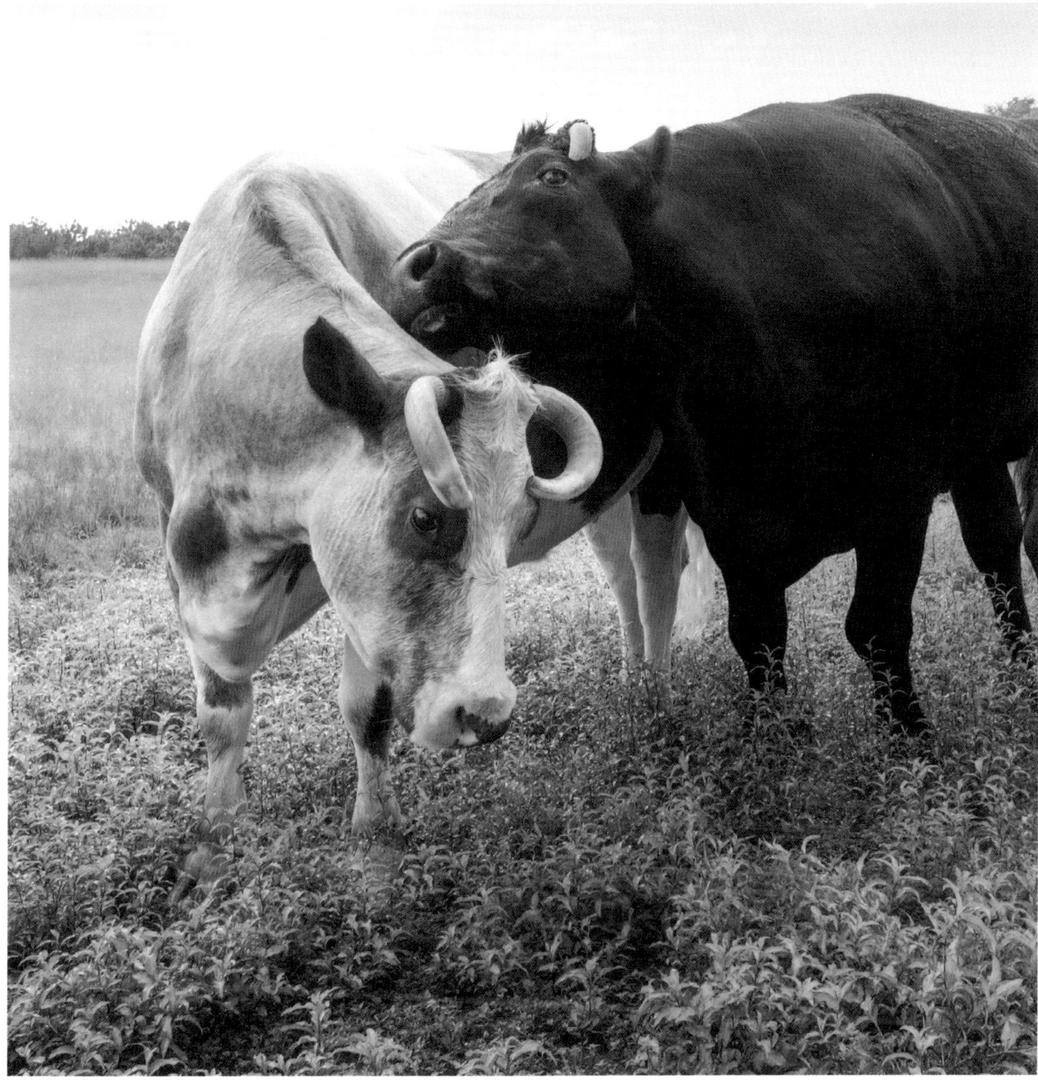

Ainsley *(Holstein/Scottish Highland mix) and* ***Jason***

Ainsley was intended to become a "replacement heifer" on a dairy farm. A replacement heifer is a young female cow who has been selected to join the milking herd in the future. These heifers are raised to replace older cows, whose production wanes after several years of forced pregnancies and are slaughtered.

At eight weeks of age, Ainsley developed an umbilical hernia that went untreated and continued to grow. The farmer gave her up because he "would not get anything for her" at auction.

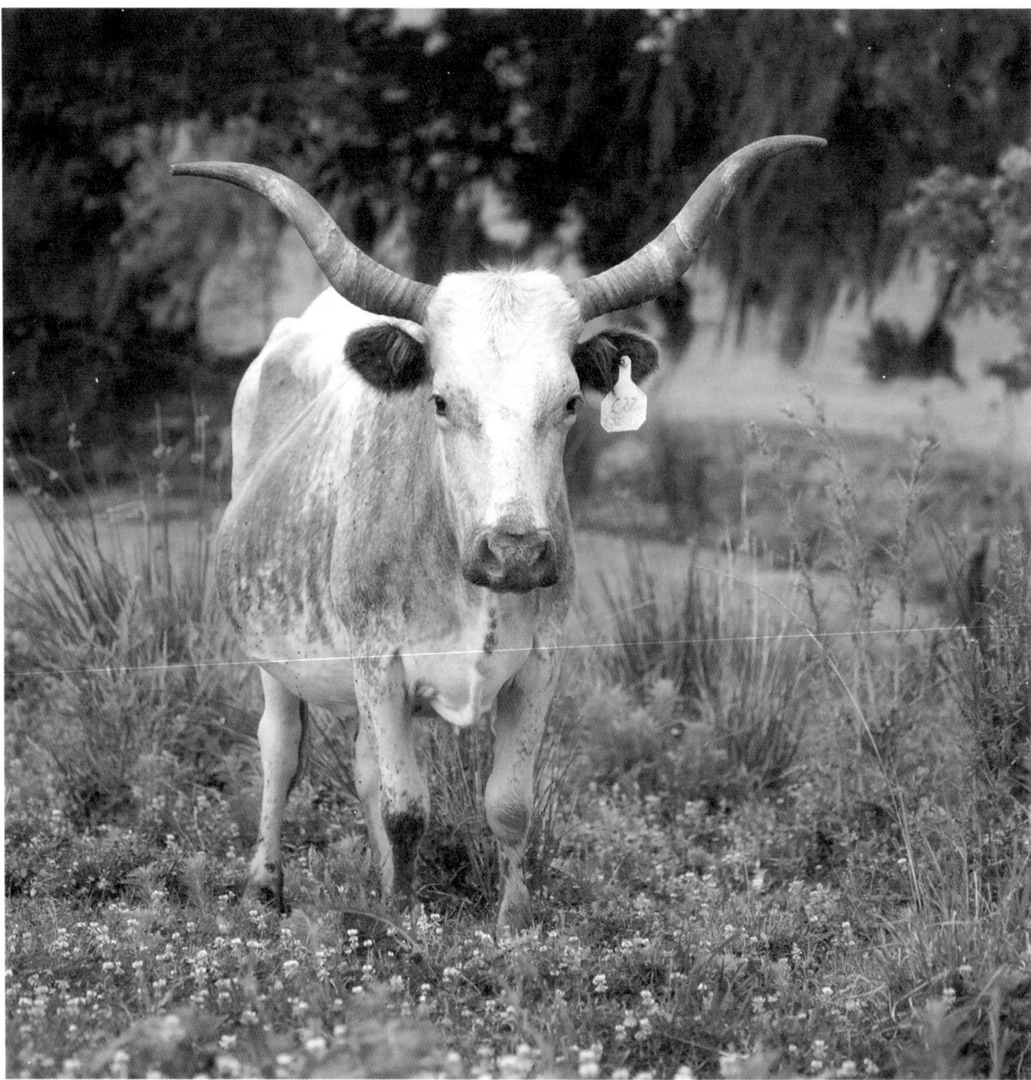

***Sunrise** (Longhorn)*

Sunrise was rescued in a group of forty cows from an extreme cruelty situation. She arrived in a sanctuary pregnant with her daughter, Connie. *See "Sunrise Moos: The Tale of a Rescued Herd" on page 113.*

Why do some cows still have ear tags? Sanctuaries prioritize the well-being of the animals, and decisions about ear tags are made based on what is best for each individual animal's health and comfort. Removing ear tags can be painful and stressful for the animals. If the tags are not causing harm or discomfort, it's often kinder to leave them in place.

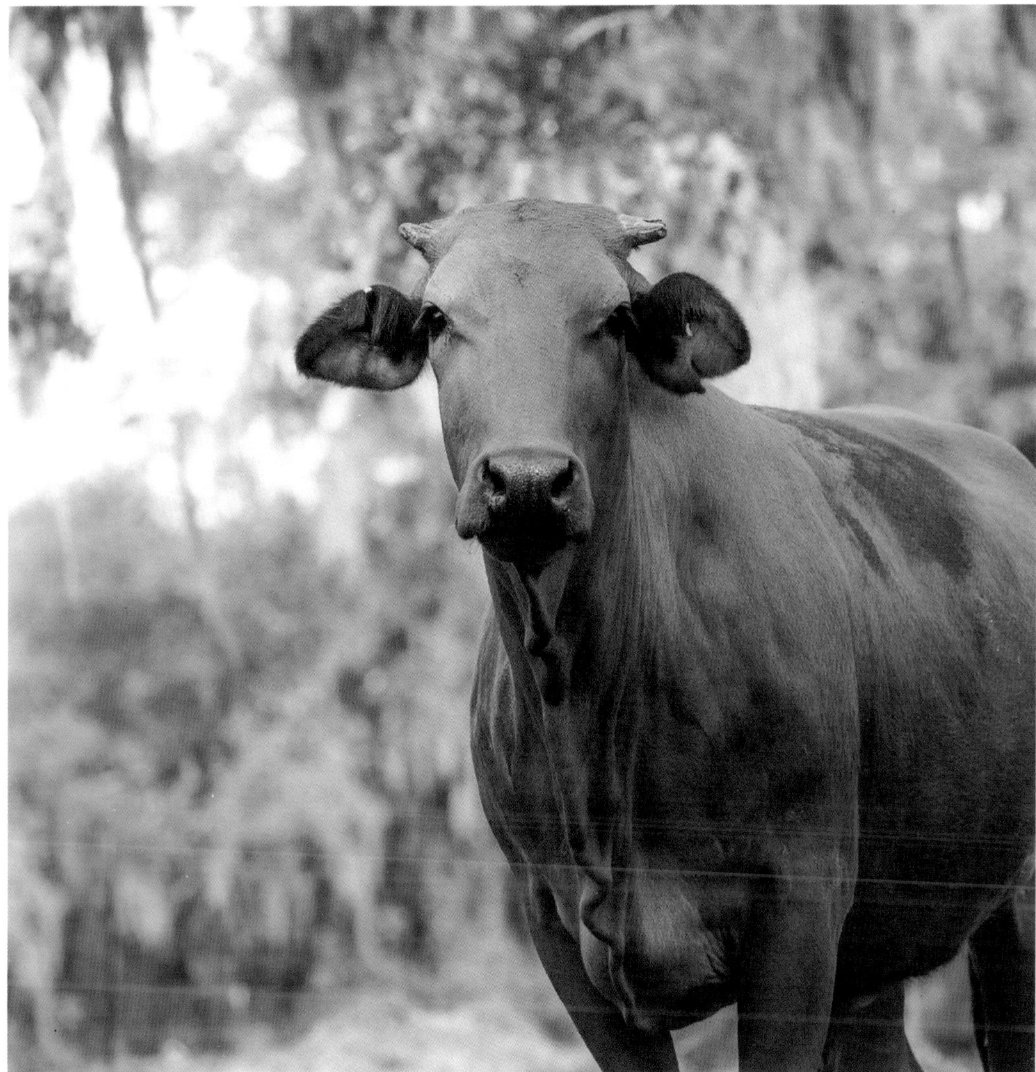

***Jingles** (Brahman)*

When Jingles was born, her mother didn't produce any milk, so the farm asked a worker to bottle-raise the calf. The same worker simultaneously raised another heifer, Bella, whose mom had passed away. The worker developed a deep bond with the calves, and she convinced the farmer to allow both to go to a sanctuary. The pair remain best friends. When Jingles sprained her ankle and had to be isolated for a few days, Bella stood outside the pen and bellowed to be let in.

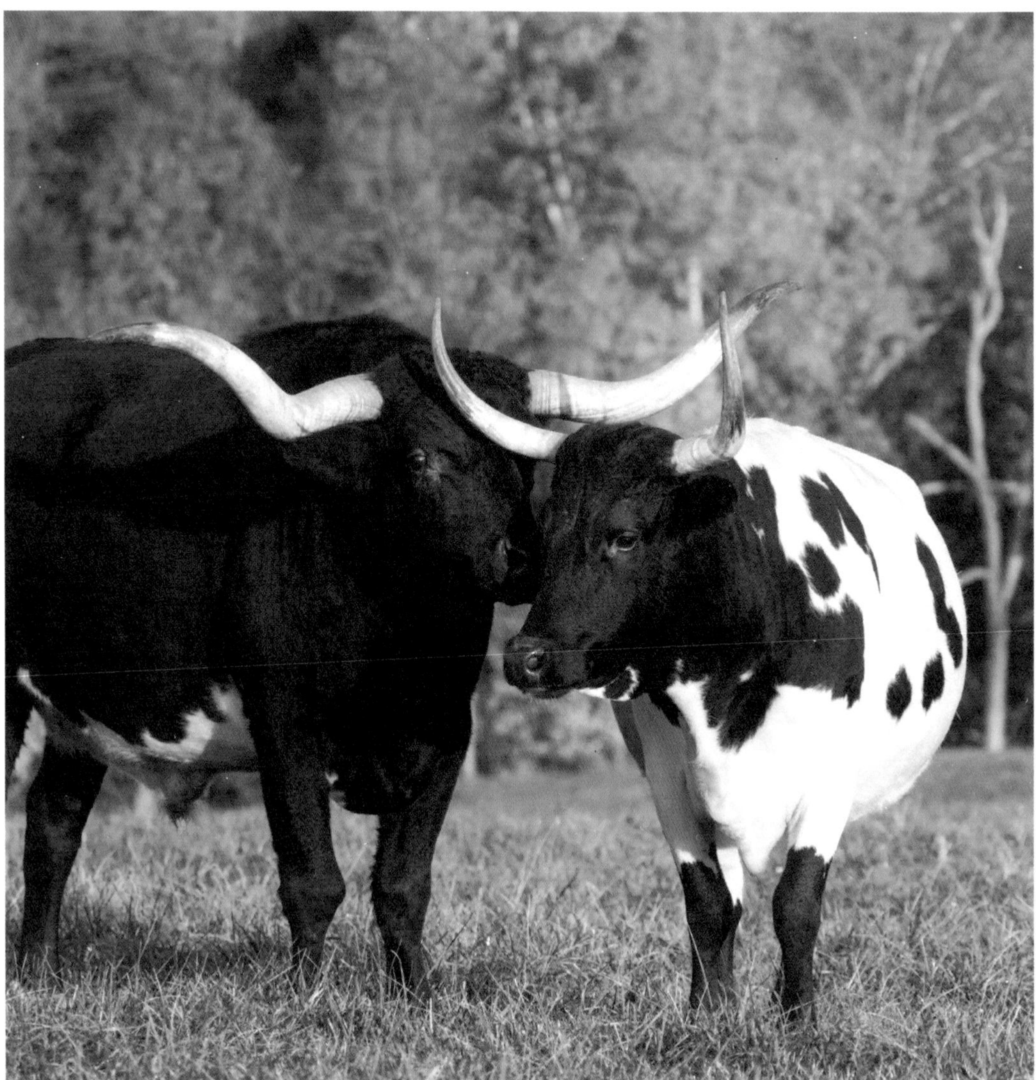

Mini Moo *(Longhorn) and* ***Lucy*** *(Longhorn)*

A man brought a sickly calf to a butcher shop to be slaughtered, but the owner said he was too small and told him to "fatten him up" first. A compassionate woman ran after the owner in the parking lot and bought the calf for a few dollars, saving his life. She named him Mini Moo, and cared for him until her family sold their farm.

Lucy gave birth while awaiting slaughter. She and her newborn lay in a kill pen for three days until a horse rescuer saved them. The calf needed hospital care, but he was later reunited with Lucy in a sanctuary, safe at last.

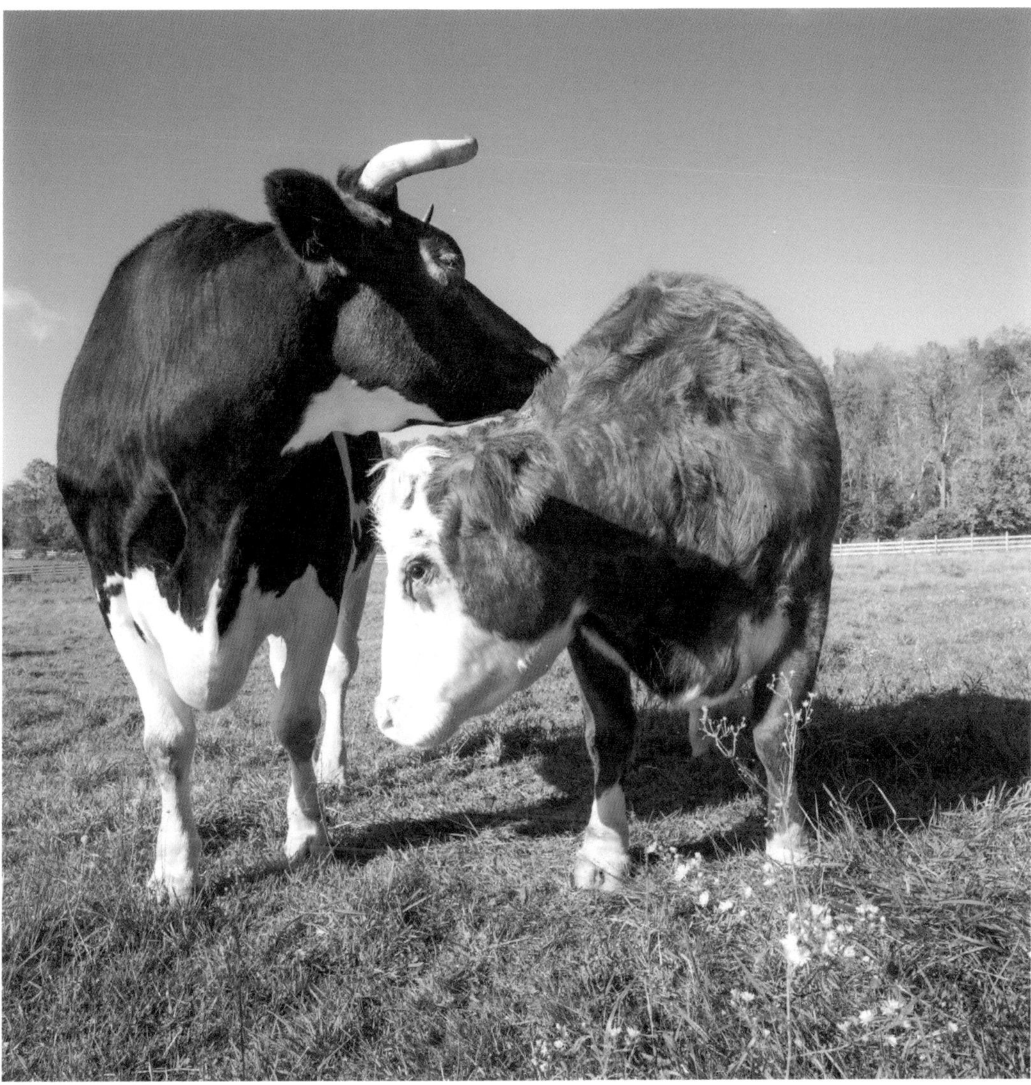

Rupert *(Holstein) and* ***Jimmy*** *(Hereford)*

On the drive to her prom, a young woman spotted Rupert on the side of the road—a tiny, unrecognizable bundle of fur covered in road rash. Stooping down in her prom dress, she discovered a calf in desperate need of saving. Likely, he fell from a veal calf transport truck. Instead of going to prom, this incredible girl took Rupert home and gave him the care he desperately needed. Thanks to the nurturing care of her and her family, Rupert grew healthy and strong.

Jimmy and his mother, PennyLove, were rescued from a beef farm.

SAFE HAVEN FARM SANCTUARY

Bill and Ellen Crain, Co-Founders, and the Sanctuary Staff
Poughquag, New York

Ethel and Surprise

(Photographs on pages 120 and 121)

In 2008, we opened Safe Haven Farm Sanctuary in Upstate New York. The sanctuary provides a lifelong home for rescued farmed animals. We didn't have enough pasture for cows then, but eleven years later we moved down the road to a larger property. Our first two cows were Ethel and her daughter, Surprise, aged nineteen and thirteen.

The cows came from a small dairy farm run by a husband and wife. The husband died, and the wife had physical problems that prevented her from taking over the farm. She made the heartbreaking decision to sell their land and rehome their beloved cows. She sold them all except Ethel and Surprise. The couple had developed a special fondness for these two, and she wanted them to stay together. But no farm would take a cow of Ethel's age, which is about as long as cows ordinarily live. After an extensive search, the woman found us, and we agreed to adopt the pair.

When Ethel arrived, our vet detected a growth on her eye, and suspected cancer behind it. He didn't give her long to live. But three years later, mother and daughter are both active and clearly loving life.

Ethel and Surprise are tightly bonded. Surprise can often be seen licking her mother's face with affection and adoration. But we found that mother and daughter have very different personalities.

While Ethel doesn't seek out attention from humans, she is approachable and gentle. Surprise, in contrast, tends to distrust humans and is short-tempered. We quickly learned that if we got too close to her, she would bang us with a jerk of her head. We knew that if she really wanted to, she could hurt us badly, so we gave her space in which to feel more comfortable. Over time, Surprise has become more accustomed to us and even seems to have developed a degree of trust in us, so we don't have to be quite so vigilant.

During the next year, we adopted six more cows, both females and males. Cows live in a matriarchal society, led by a strong female. Ethel became the matriarch of our herd. As new cows joined it, Ethel was very attentive to them. For example, one cow arrived at the sanctuary and seemed disoriented when she walked out of the transport truck. Ethel walked beside her to the barn, seeming to assure her that the barn was her home.

One night, one of us (Bill) experienced Ethel's matriarchal presence firsthand:

> I was walking down a steep hill after checking a water trough. A calf who weighed about 400 pounds ran up to meet me, eager to play. I was startled. My footing was poor, and I was afraid he would knock me down. I shouted several times for him to stop, but he persisted. Then I heard heavy footsteps behind me. It was Ethel. She looked at me and the calf for about a minute, then lumbered back down the hill. She had apparently come to make sure that everything was all right. Her presence influenced the calf, who became a bit more restrained, allowing me to walk back down.

Ethel frequently inserts herself when she senses drama, diffusing the situation. She doesn't actually do much in a physical way; she simply looks at those involved. It's as if she is saying, "Behave yourselves; Mother is watching."

Romeo

(Photograph on page 53)

Romeo was brought to us by a woman whose boyfriend owns a dairy farm. He, like other dairy farmers, doesn't allow the male calves to live long. This is because the males cannot produce milk. Many are killed soon after birth, while others, raised for veal, are slaughtered after a few months.

The woman was very upset by this system. To maintain their relationship, she and her boyfriend reached an agreement: If she could find a lifelong home for a newborn male, he would release his ownership of the calf to the new farm.

The woman was thrilled that we would adopt Romeo, but she didn't bring him to us right away. Born four weeks prematurely, he was too weak to stand and needed special care.

When he was two weeks old, he seemed strong enough to come to us. He weighed only thirty-five pounds—less than half the weight of most full-term newborns. Our vet discovered that he hadn't recovered from an umbilical cord infection, which required us to give him daily medical treatments for two months. We also bottle fed him for two months.

We were immediately enamored of this new calf. We named him Romeo because the white spot on his forehead looked like a heart.

Romeo grew into a strong and vigorous young adult who is quite friendly toward humans. When he sees one of us, he comes over for petting and scratching. If another male acts roughly toward any human, he rushes over to provide protection. Often, he butts the cow away. We suspect that Romeo feels protective toward his human caretakers due to all the care he received when he was a sickly calf. As one of our long-time staff members says, "The animals know that we have helped them out and love us for it."

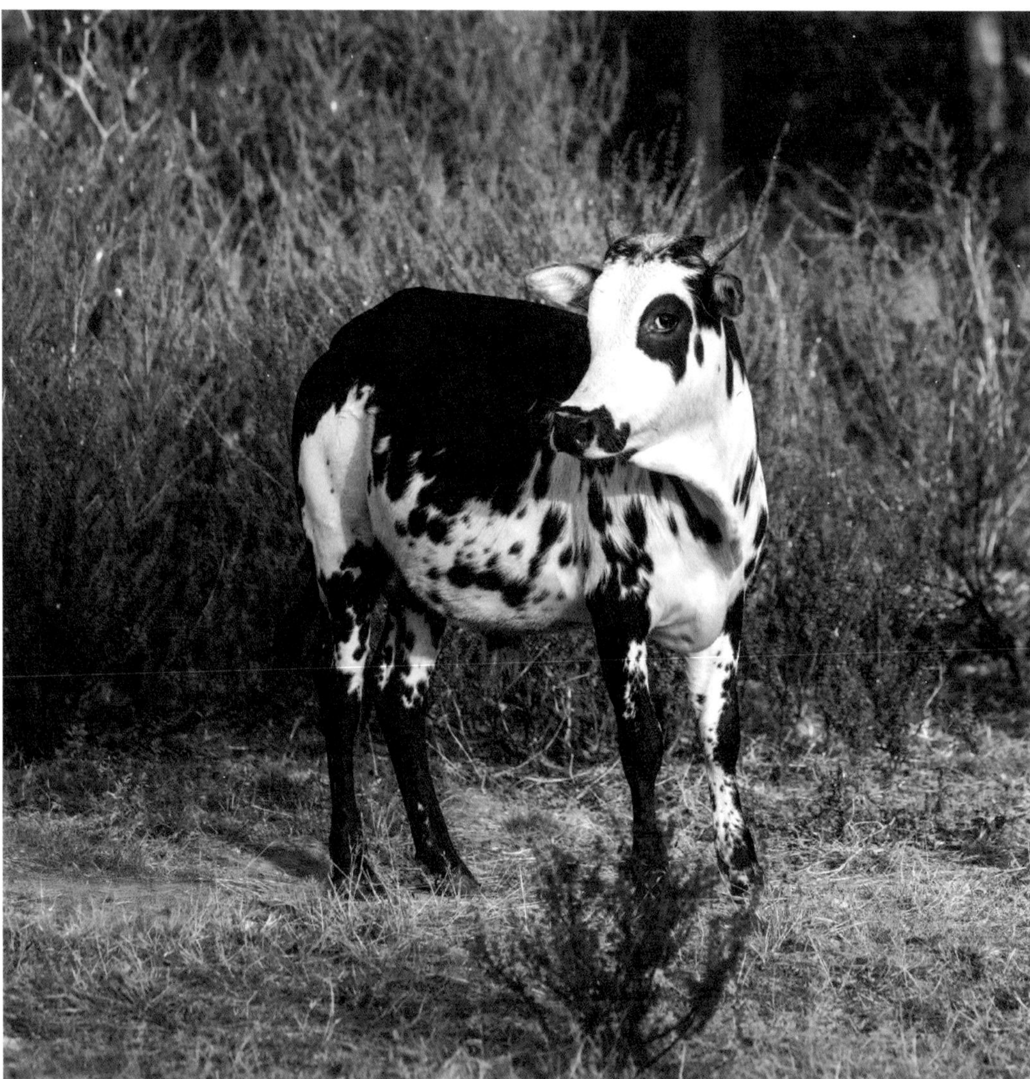

Shmoo *(Zebu)*

A small farm in the Midwestern United States did not have space available for this calf and looked for a permanent home for him. As a small cow, he now shares time with pigs, sheep, and other smaller animals in a sanctuary.

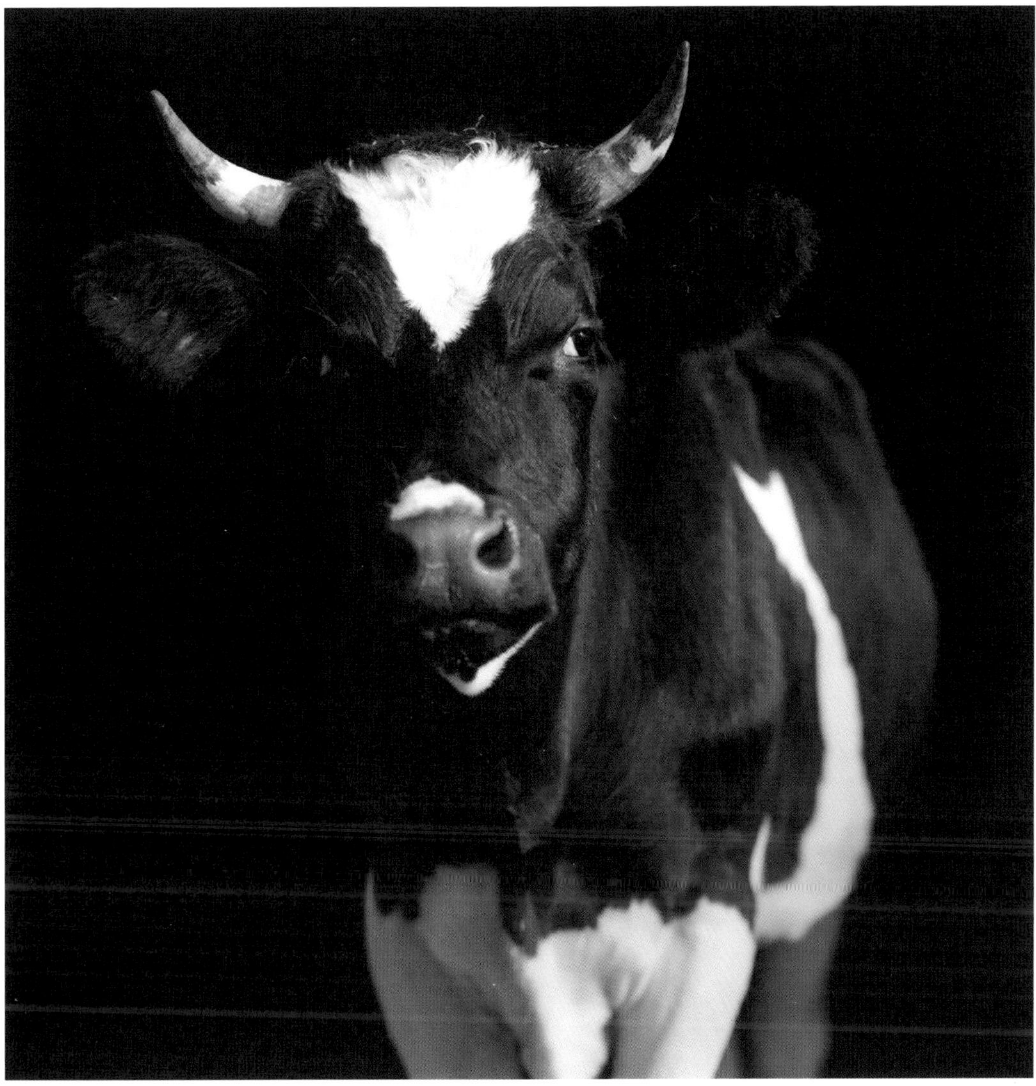

Romeo *(Holstein)*
Romeo was born four weeks prematurely on a dairy farm. *See "Romeo" on page 50.*

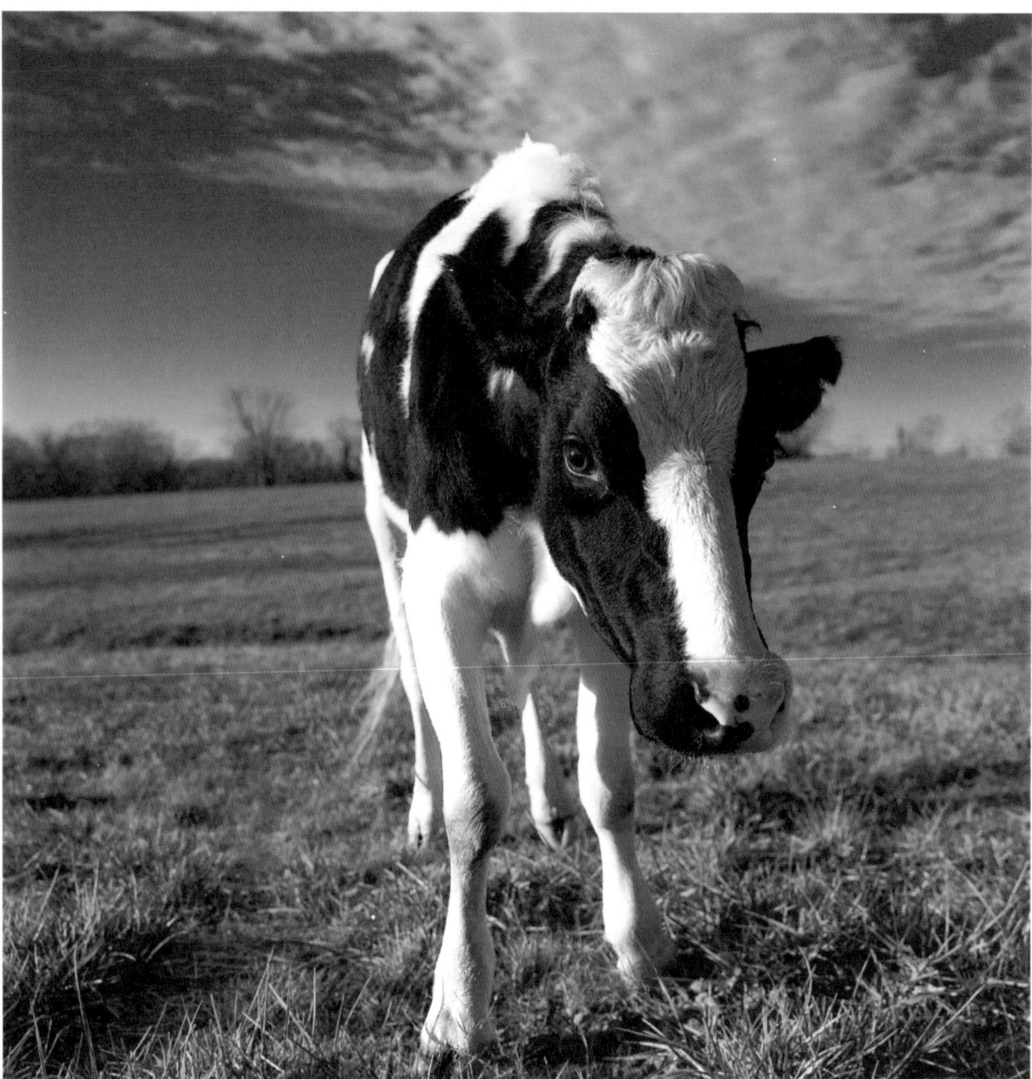

Remi *(Holstein)*

Remi was born blind on a dairy farm. The farmers contacted a sanctuary and asked them to give her a good home. The other cows help her to stay with her new herd by getting behind her and pushing gently when she falls behind. One morning, I found the herd grazing nearly a mile from their barn. The cows who had ventured farthest away? Remi and an older steer named Moses, who walked alongside her to help her navigate.

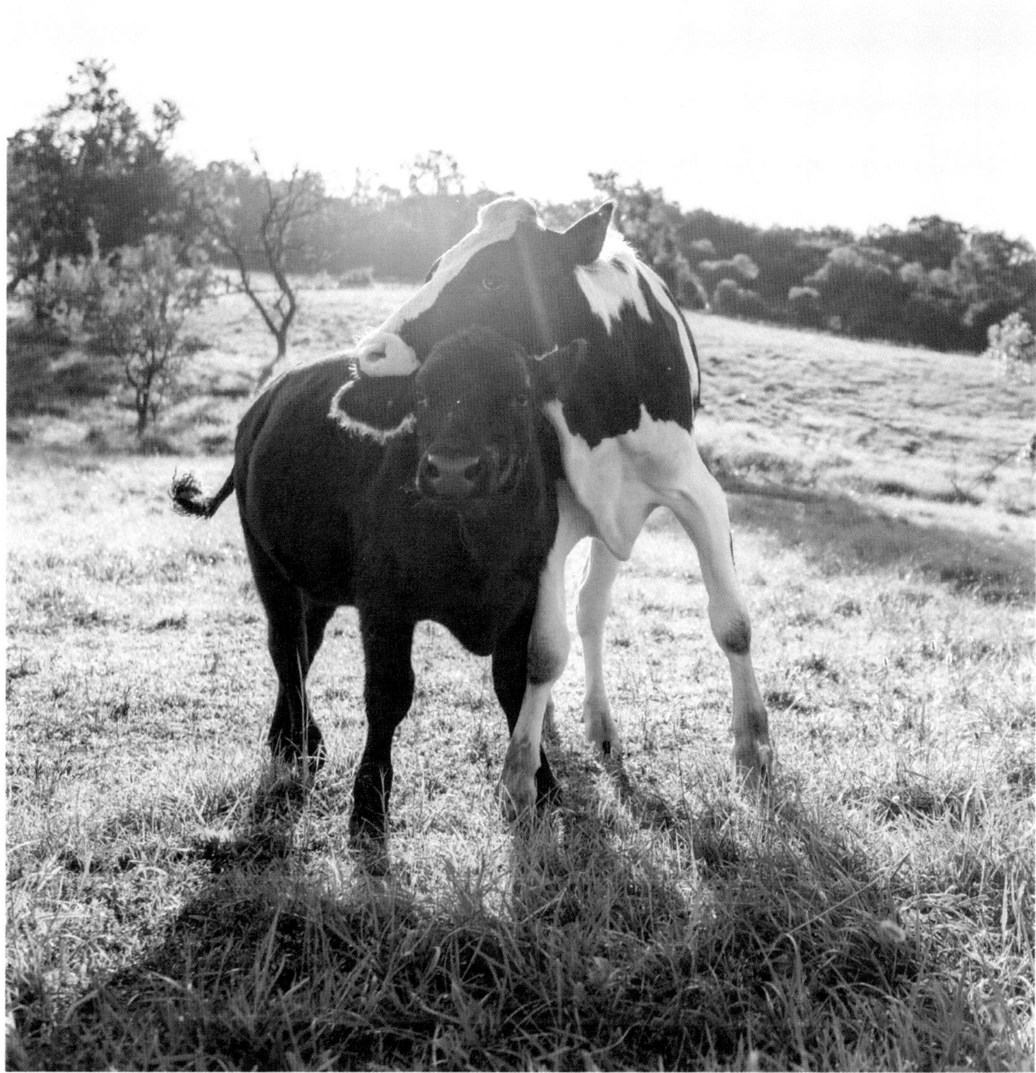

Ivy *(Angus) and* ***Remi***

Born a twin on a beef cattle farm, Ivy was so much tinier than her brother and the other young calves that she needed extra feed and help to survive in the cow herd. The farmer's wife took care of her, and in the process fell in love with her, and didn't want to see her killed. In a sanctuary, she and Remi are best friends.

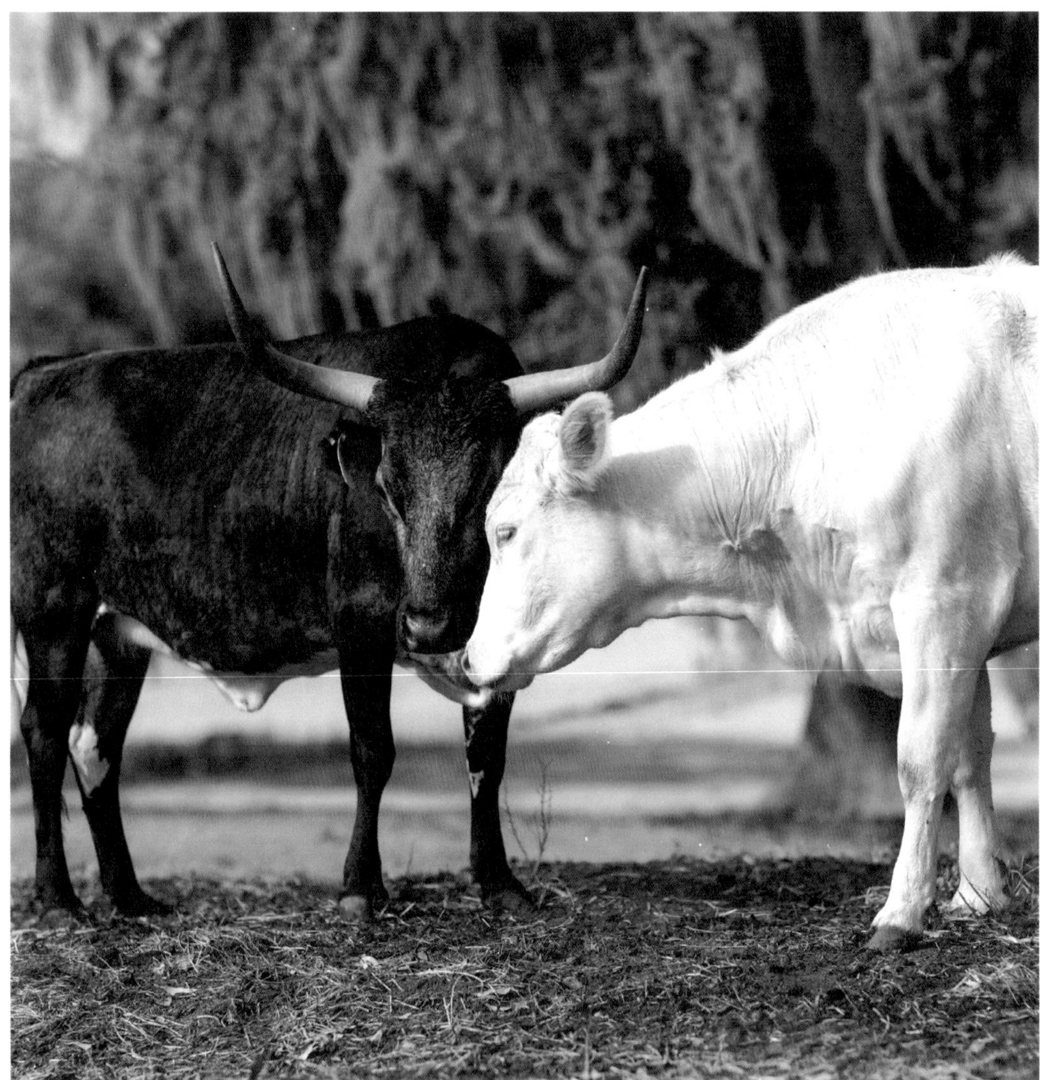

Cécile *(Longhorn) and* ***Amie*** *(Longhorn)*

Mother and daughter were rescued in a group of forty cows from an extreme cruelty situation. *See "Sunrise Moos: The Tale of a Rescued Herd" on page 113.*

Gaining trust from traumatized animals is challenging. They don't understand treats or gentle touches, associating humans with only pain and grief. As these animals have no prior experience with kindness, building trust, when it happens at all, requires time and patience.

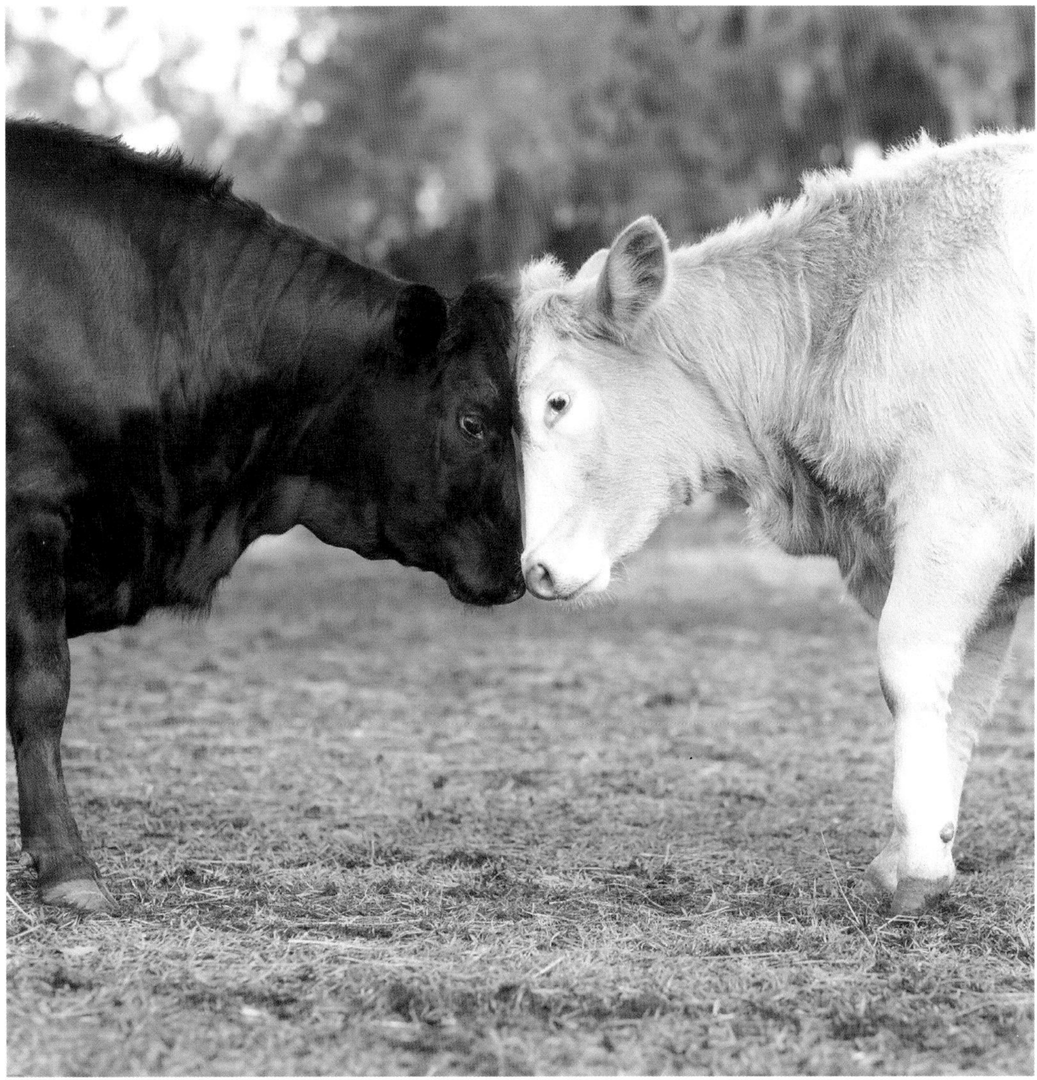

Terri *(Dexter) and* ***Duchess Gracelyn Adalind Holland Van der Moo*** *(Brangus mix)*

Terri and Duchess's mothers were rescued from an extreme cruelty case and arrived at the sanctuary pregnant with these girls. See "Sunrise Moos: The Tale of a Rescued Herd" on page 113.

One day, staff noticed Duchess limping—she had injured her knee and needed care. But as one of the herd's smartest cows, she evaded every attempt to quarantine her for healing.

After weeks of recovery, she decided she was ready and escaped—simply opening the gate herself. Staff later found her back in the pasture, happily reunited with her herd.

INDRALOKA ANIMAL SANCTUARY

By Indra Lahiri, Founder
Dalton, Pennsylvania

Moksha: Liberation Through Love

(Photograph on page 64)

The trembling calf cowered in the brush, peeking out cautiously. Tempted by the promise of a bottle, he emerged and suckled hungrily, each gulp reverberating through the silence. He was a shadow of what he should have been, stunted by malnourishment and trauma. His red coat lacked luster, with patches of hair missing along his bony spine. Fleas and lice crawled all over him, causing constant discomfort, while flies buzzed around him like an unending nuisance. Manure clung to his tail, a testament to the neglect he had endured. He was little more than a skeleton, every bone visible beneath his fragile skin.

But oh, his eyes! Big, round, deep brown pools of longing and fear, gazing through his beautiful long lashes. Even as he suckled the bottle, he watched warily, ready to flee at the faintest hint of danger. In his short, painful month on earth, he had already learned not to trust humans.

In the car on the way home, he tentatively leaned into my touch, the warmth of his frail body contrasting with the cool metal around us.

Gradually, his need for affection overcame his fear, and he nestled his head on my lap, sighing with relief, as the rumble of the engine drowned out the echoes of his past. We christened him Moksha, meaning liberation, for in our embrace, he would find freedom from the chains of suffering that had bound him.

A cow named Penny, wise and weathered, awaited him at the sanctuary, a beacon of solace in a chaotic world. She had known loss, having felt the ache of separation as each of her own calves was stolen from her just after birth. But now she would nurture Moksha as her own, offering him the love and warmth he craved.

Their meeting brought tears to Penny's eyes, each a memory of the babies she had lost and the sorrow lingering in her soul. As Moksha tentatively approached, drawn by the promise of a mother's embrace, she enveloped him, her heart swelling with a love beyond words.

Despite having been at the sanctuary, away from any bulls, for years, Penny began to lactate. She nursed Moksha, saving him from starvation.

Yet their bond was not without trials. Penny's aging body faltered. Nursing a calf at her age proved too much. She developed a life-threatening infection in her teats and was no longer able to nurse Moksha. He grew depressed and refused to eat.

Day after day, Penny grew stronger, but we couldn't risk her nursing again. Yet Moksha grew sicker, experiencing multiple digestive challenges as we bottle-fed him. And he was sad. He refused to play, showed no interest in affection, and cried for Penny.

A compassionate police officer brought Leif E. Greene to us. She had rescued the skinny little goat from a dark, dirty garage, where he was tied up. Children taunted him, throwing rocks, and he had no escape. The person who had called in the complaint stated that this had been going on for months. No wonder this little guy didn't trust humans.

Leif took one look at Moksha and decided they were new best friends. He pranced over to him and invited him to a hearty game of tag. The next morning, Moksha ate solid food for the first time. By the second day, his digestive problems had disappeared. The calf and goat played all day long, until they fell asleep in a heap like puppies.

A few days later, Leif looked me in the eye and smiled. Progress! This precious little being, on the strength of love and play, was saving Moksha's life, and had a heart so open he was willing to give humans another chance. Soon, Leif was dancing with joy every time he saw us. He even began to leap over his fence to find us anywhere on the property, demanding that we play with him and Moksha. In the mornings, as I fed Moksha his bottle, Leif pranced joyfully in circles around us, stopping occasionally to kiss Moksha or me. He was actually celebrating Moksha's care! This little goat stole my heart, and I felt it would burst for the love of such a giving soul.

Moksha flourished, his frail form strengthened by the love surrounding him, his spirit uplifted by those who saw his worth. Children and adults flocked to him, drawn by the gentle wisdom in his eyes, pouring out their hearts to a creature who listened with unwavering patience, his gaze reflecting their deepest selves. As he embraced them, they found solace, reassured that all would be well.

Four months passed. One day, Leif seemed like a healthy, joyful goat that would be with us for years to come. The next day, his kidneys shut down, and then his heart stopped. We don't know why. The vets don't know why. We rushed him to the hospital, but there was nothing they could do.

His time with us was invaluable, if all too brief. Our sweet little angel died in our arms, knowing he was much beloved, and that we were sorry to see him go.

We feared that Moksha would plunge back into the darkness of his early losses, but the rest of the cows, many of the cats, goats, and humans all poured love into him. He thrived, growing big and strong and confident, with a playful side.

Moksha also developed depth. His early struggles seemed to make it easier for him to recognize when another being of any species was hurting. He's become a favorite among visitors, greeting them with kindness and instilling them with the light of love. Children and adults alike visit him, their hearts heavy with the burdens of their own lives. In his presence, they find solace, their fears melting away beneath the warmth of his gaze. And as he wraps his neck around them in a tender embrace, they feel a sense of peace wash over them, a reminder that even in the darkest of times there is light to be found.

For Moksha is more than a cow: he embodies hope, a light in a world shrouded in darkness.

As the sun dipped below the horizon and the shadows grew long, Moksha stood amidst the rustling leaves, his heart full of the gift of memories and the promise of tomorrow. Beside him, Rupert, once a tiny orphaned calf, now towered over him, his frame stretched tall and proud against the backdrop of the setting sun.

From the moment Rupert arrived at the sanctuary, he and Moksha and Marble, a lamb with eyes as bright as the morning dew, formed an inseparable bond. Together, they roamed the fields, their laughter mingling with the gentle hum of the breeze.

One memorable day, the sanctuary hosted an event for humans, a celebration of life and love amidst the rolling hills and sprawling fields. As the guests lined up for the buffet, Rupert and Marble, with a mischievous twinkle in their eyes, joined the queue, their manners impeccable as they waited their turn.

When they reached the salad bar, they indulged in the crisp greens with gusto, their appetite matched only by their sense of adventure. Within moments, they consumed the entire salad, meant for one hundred people. We couldn't help but laugh, though. They were so pleased.

Another cow, named Jimmy, with his humor and energy, became another close companion to Moksha, infusing joy into their days, turning the mundane into the extraordinary through silly antics like wearing the huge, heavy hay feeder around his neck like a necklace, prancing around the pasture as we raced to catch up, afraid he would catch it on something and hurt himself.

Jimmy, Rupert, and especially Moksha have been like doting uncles to Beau and Bear, two calves rescued this past year. They've spent countless hours playing with them, ensuring their safety, and teaching them the ways of sanctuary life. When Beau and Bear were tiny, Moksha, Rupert, and Jimmy made sure they were always surrounded by the adult cows for protection.

Mini MiniMonkey, a tiny cat with a curved tail and a heart of gold, also found solace in Moksha's gentle presence. Together, they explored the sanctuary, their footsteps a symphony of silence in the stillness of the night.

During the day, they ran amidst the tall grasses, their laughter echoing through the trees as they chased each other in playful abandon. And when the cold winds blew and the stars shone bright, Mini MiniMonkey curled up beside Moksha, her warmth a balm to his sweet soul.

Their friendship was a testament to the power of love, a reminder that even in the darkest of times, there is light to be found. And as they watched the sun rise each morning, they knew that together, they could weather any storm that came their way.

The years passed, each one bringing new challenges and triumphs to the inhabitants of the sanctuary. Moksha grew older, his once-frail frame now huge and solid. But his spirit remained as innocent as when he was a calf, his eyes still shining with the same gentle wisdom that had drawn so many to his side.

As the sun dips below the horizon, casting long shadows over the sanctuary, Moksha stands amidst the rustling leaves, a symbol of resilience and hope. Beside him, Rupert, Marble, Jimmy, Mini MiniMonkey, and many other loved ones, their spirits intertwined in a tapestry of shared experiences and shared dreams. Moksha's heart overflowed with freedom and the joy of being.

And so the sanctuary thrives, echoing with laughter and the whisper of the wind. Moksha stands tall, his heart filled with joy, his spirit soaring on wings of hope.

In the end, it's not the darkness that defines us, but the light within. As Moksha gazes upon the world, his eyes alight with a thousand stars, he knows he is home, surrounded by enduring love.

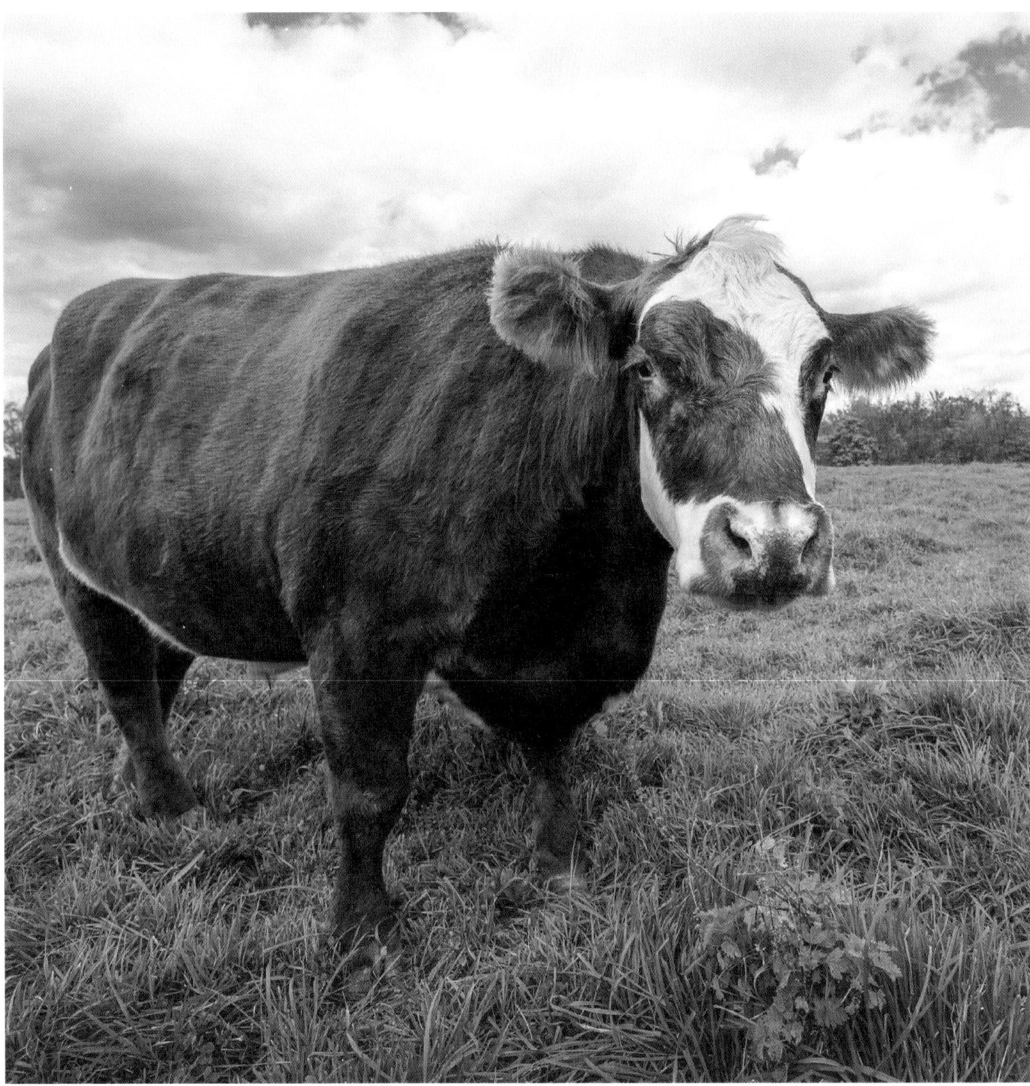

***Moksha** (Hereford)*

As a newborn calf born on an organic farm, Moksha was orphaned when his mother was sent to slaughter. The farmer had not realized she had given birth. The calf lay alone in a field, unknown and hungry. *See "Moksha: Liberation through Love" on page 59.*

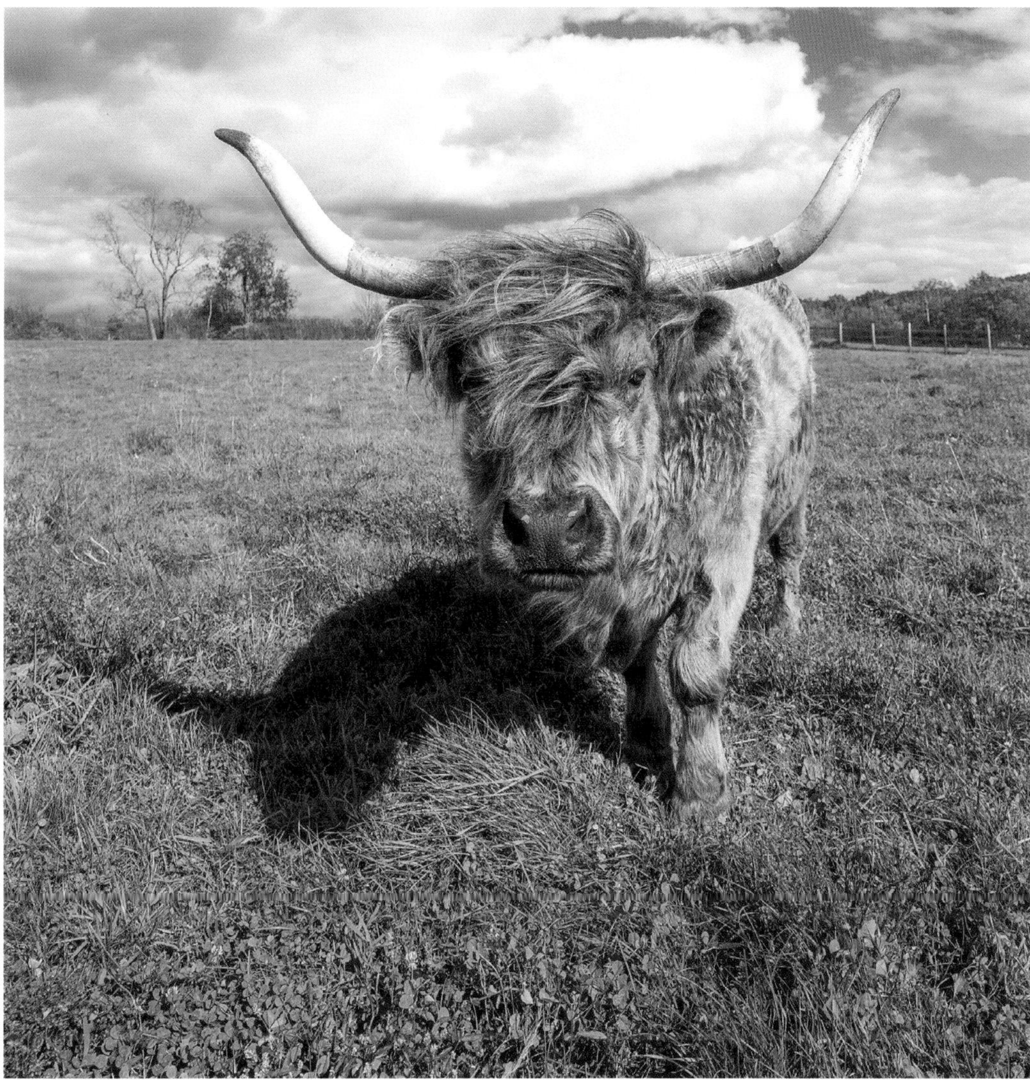

***Snuffleupagus** (Scottish Highland)*

"Gus" was the sole member of a herd destined for slaughter who could be saved. The farmer had decided to get out of the business and lease the natural gas on his property. He was going to send the entire herd to slaughter. A sanctuary was able to negotiate the release of this single cow.

Now, Gus keeps a watchful eye on the sanctuary through her shaggy bangs. She even has her own cat friends. Boo and Jinx regularly come and spend time with her.

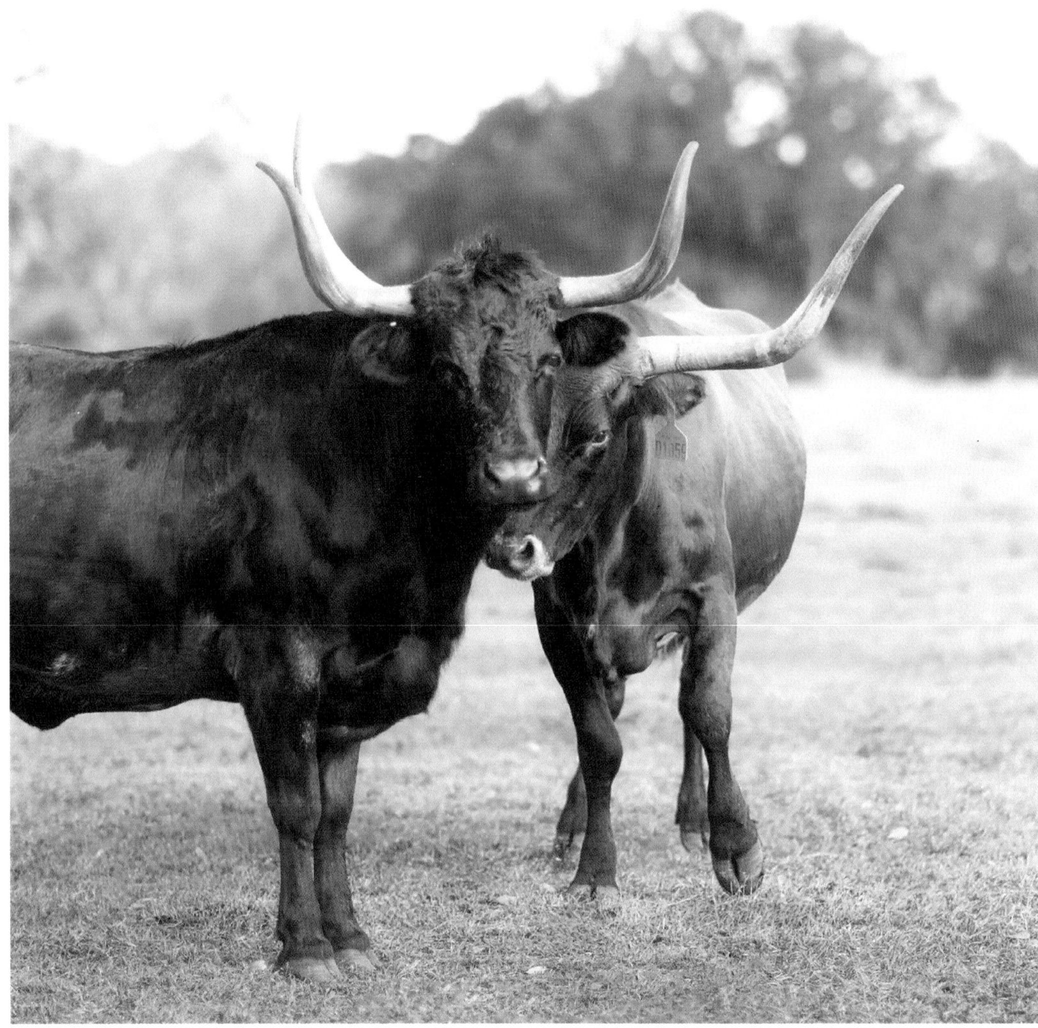

Gretchen *(Longhorn) and* **Nova** *(Longhorn)*

A cattle rancher wanted to exit the business without sending his herd to slaughter. One sanctuary accepted Gretchen, her daughter, Maia, and Maia's daughter, Serafina.

In this photo, Gretchen nuzzles Nova, a cow rescued separately from Sunrise, Florida, who bears physical scars from branding and emotional scars from mistreatment. *See "Sunrise Moos: The Tale of a Rescued Herd" on page 113.* *Friendships with their own kind help animals heal in ways that even care from the most compassionate human caretakers cannot.*

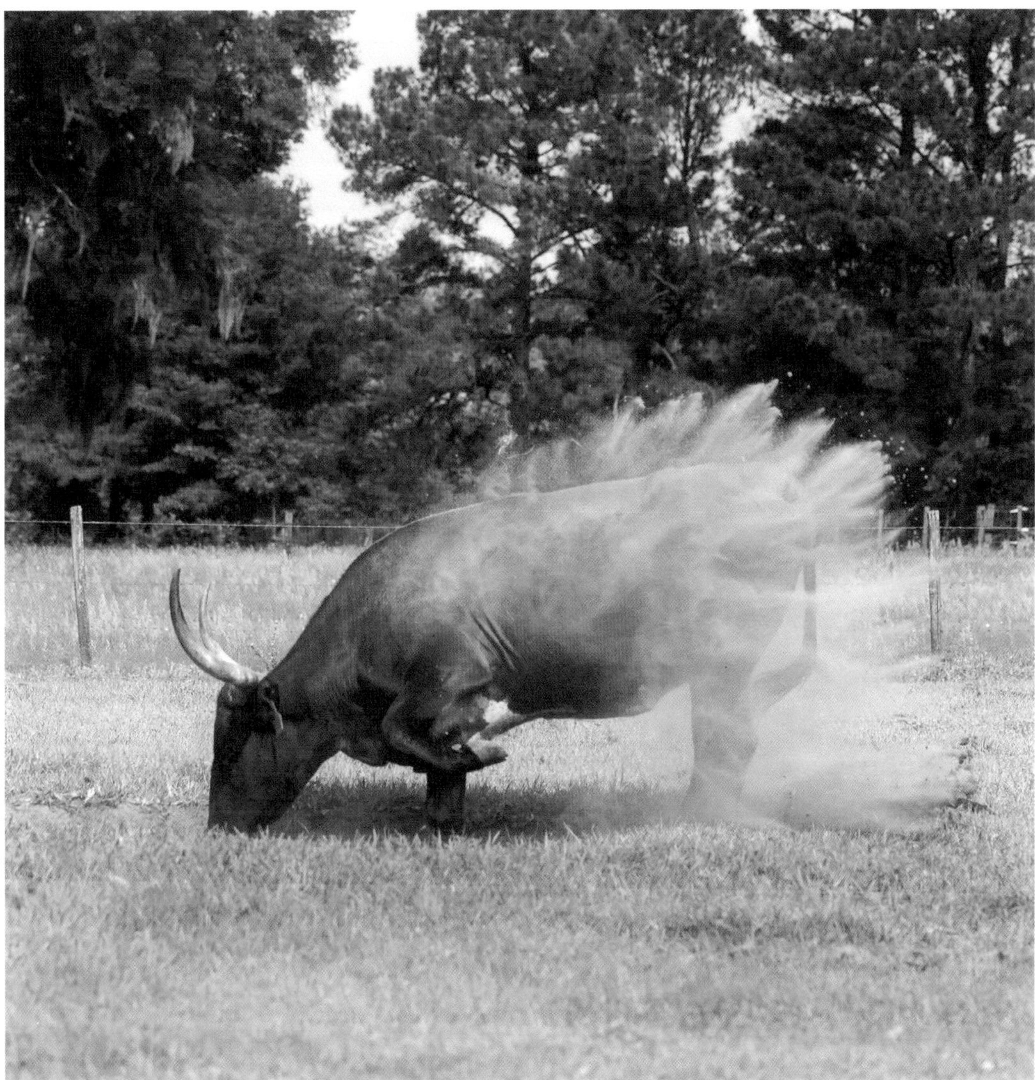

Nova

Nova kicks up dirt. One side of her body (not shown) is marked with a large branding scar that developed a mass of hypertrophic scar tissue. A veterinarian needed to remove the mass twice before the wound finally healed. Understandably, Nova neither likes nor trusts humans.

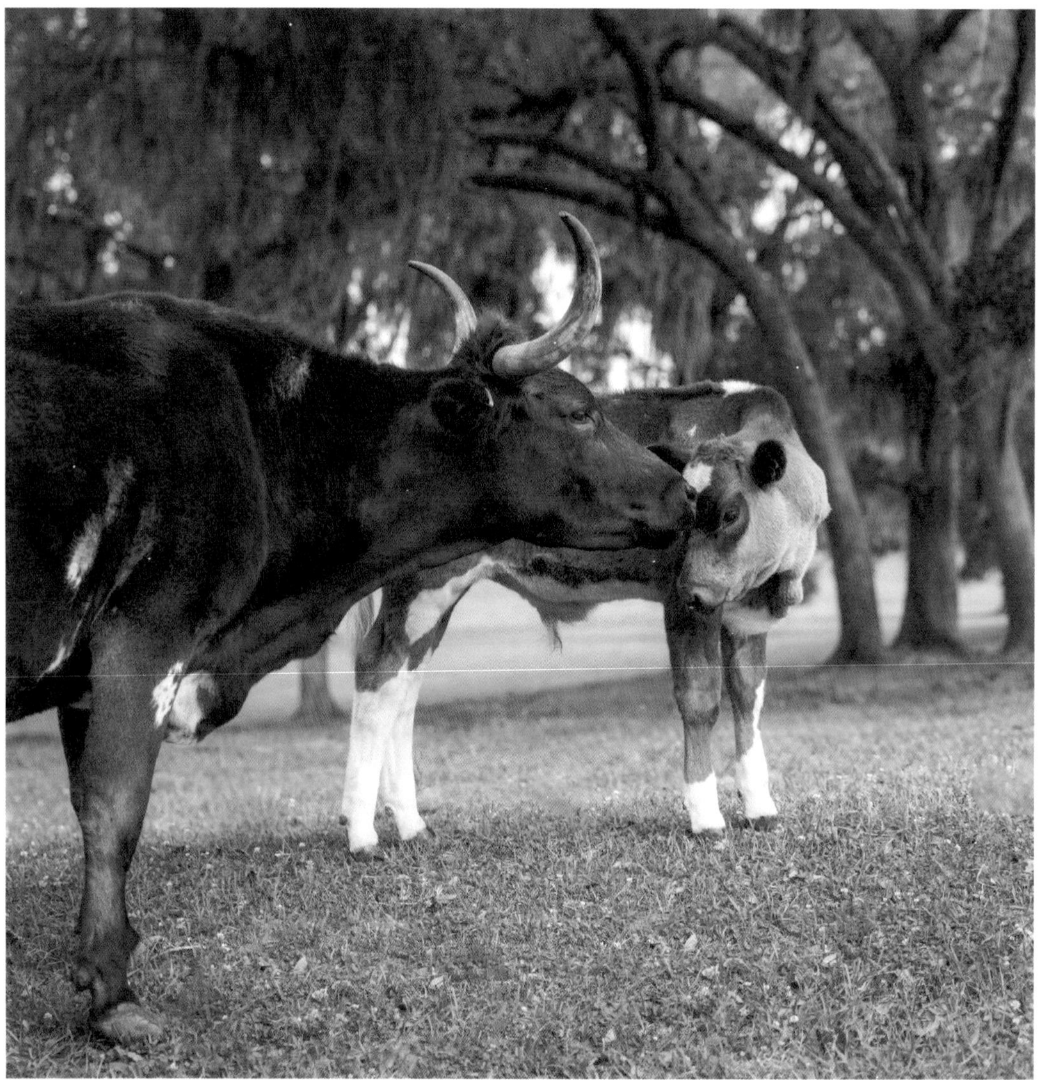

***Maia** (Longhorn) and **Zeus Amadeus Mozart** (Longhorn)*

When a cattle ranch closed, a sanctuary gave several of the cows a home, including Gretchen (previous page spread), her daughter, Maia, and Maia's daughter, Serafina. Both younger cows arrived pregnant.

Maia gave birth to Zeus Amadeus Mozart ("ZAM"), and about six weeks later, Serafina delivered Quattro—ZAM's nephew.

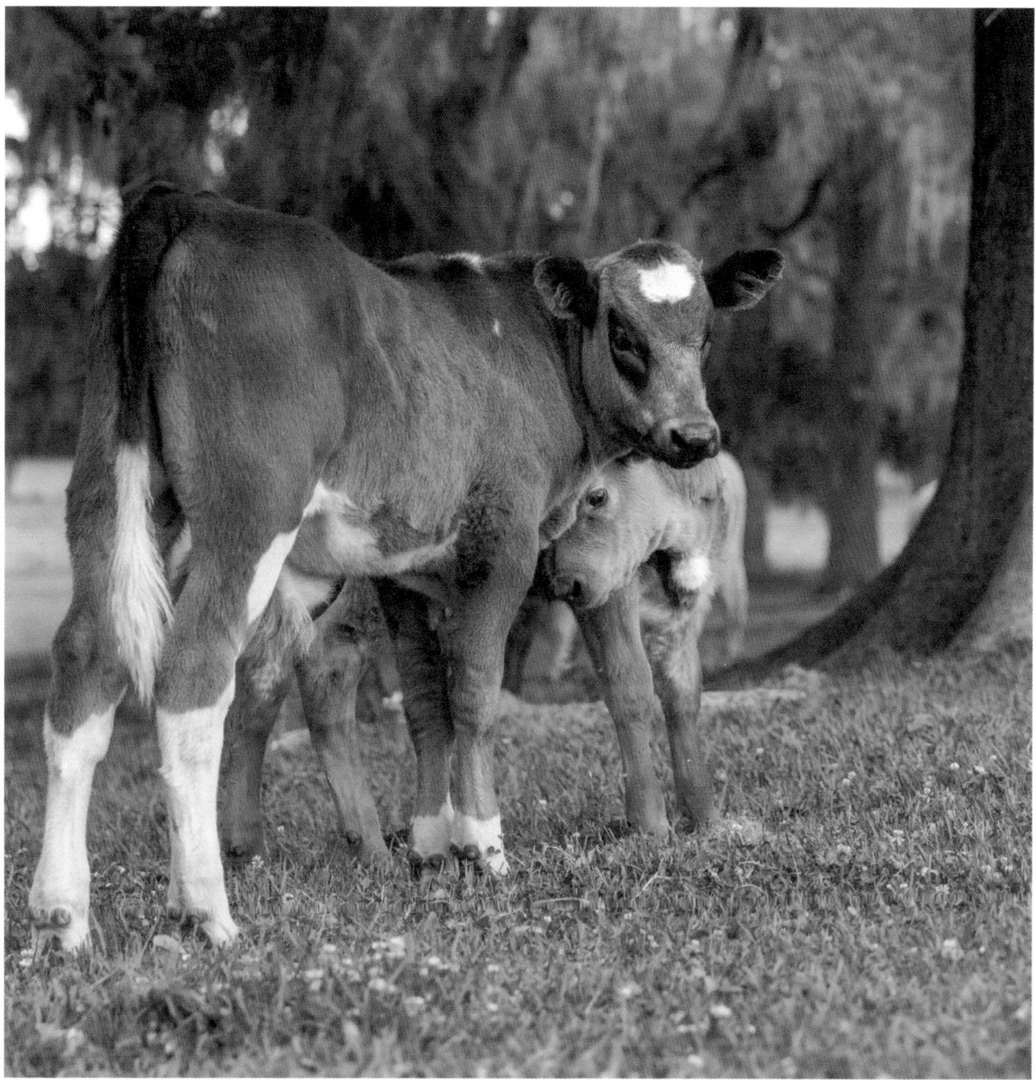

Zeus Amadeus Mozart *and* ***Quattro*** *(Longhorn)*

Quattro plays with his uncle ZAM. Both are only a few months old and are growing up together. ZAM is protective of the younger calf.

Great-grandma Gretchen and grandma Maia often "babysit" Quattro while his mother, Serafina, grazes.

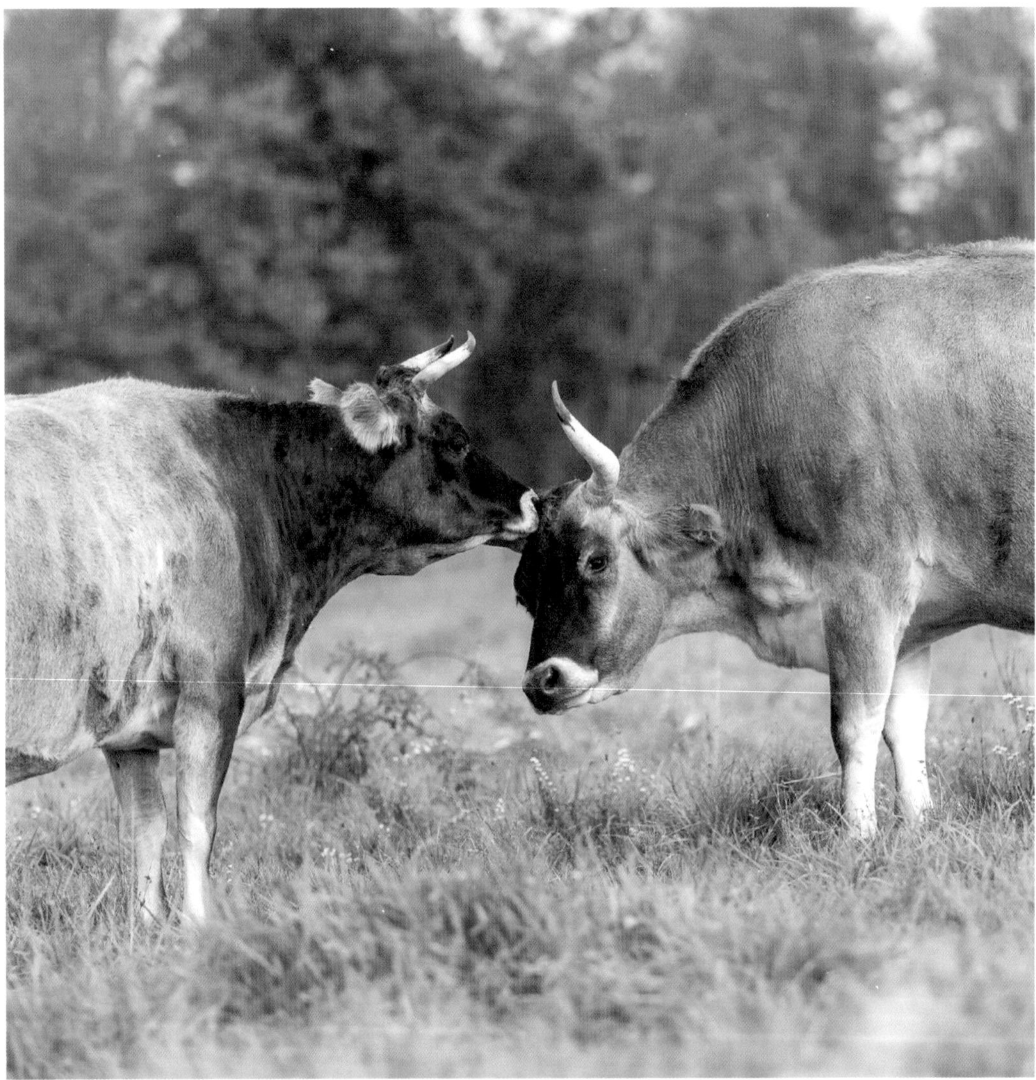

Rachel *(Jersey) and* ***Diraj*** *(Jersey)*

A group of doctors visiting a "humane" farm discovered Rachel, Diraj, and two more calves were destined for veal crates and negotiated the cows' freedom. Years later, these four cows can often be seen grooming each other and curling up together.

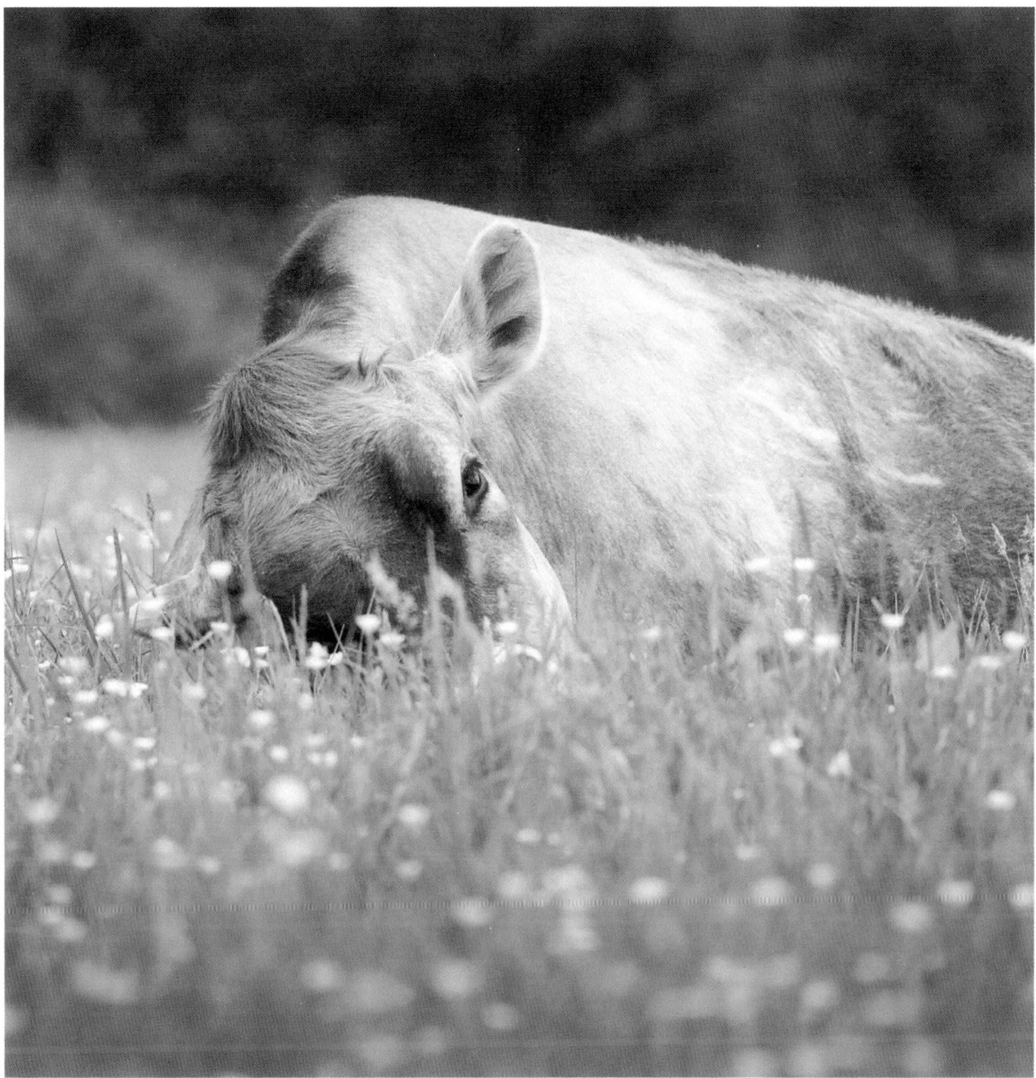

Jonathan *(Jersey)*

Born on a dairy farm, Jonathan was rescued and sent to a sanctuary instead of being auctioned. When the sanctuary owner had a stroke and could no longer care for the animals, another sanctuary stepped up and provided him with a forever home.

When a sanctuary closes, others work hard to find permanent homes for the residents.

LANCASTER FARM SANCTUARY

By Sarah Salluzzo and Jonina Turzi, Co-Founders
Mount Joy, Pennsylvania

Jude

(Photographs on pages 98 and 99)

Jude was born with a cleft lip on a local dairy farm. At this dairy farm, the newborn male calves are sold once a week to a veal farmer. When this man arrived and saw Jude, with his sideways mouth and nose, he would not pay money for the calf. He said he would take him anyway, to "put him on the compost pile."

Luckily, a worker at the dairy farm stepped in. She asked the dairy farmer if she could instead find a sanctuary for Jude and contacted us. We rushed to get Jude. When we saw him, we were extremely concerned about his health—not just about his cleft lip and the risks of him aspirating, but about several signs of active infection. We took him to the veterinary hospital immediately. He was only four days old.

Jude's cleft lip turned out to be no problem. He could chew and swallow and do everything he needed to do; it just took him a little time to learn how. However, as a baby, Jude had several infections from being born on a dairy farm—bovine coronavirus, E. coli, cryptosporidiosis, and mycoplasma pneumonia. He required a lot of hospital care and even a few surgeries to remove infected bone around his jaw when he was very young. Eventually, he was well enough to come home for good!

Jude is several years old now and a big strong guy. He has not had any further trouble with infections over the years, thankfully. He is playful and sassy. We affectionately nicknamed him "StinkerBoy"! He has a fun and mischievous streak that makes him delightful to be around. There is something about Jude that has made him the center of his entire herd. He looks out for all the younger and smaller animals in his family. He has the most sensitive and intelligent eyes you could ever see. And everyone loves his perfect sideways smile too—not just because it is adorable on him, but because it saved his life.

Claire

(Photograph on page 99)

We rescued Claire from a beef farm, where she was suffering from facial paralysis. We are not sure if it occurred from trauma shortly after birth or if she was born with it. The entire right side of her face is paralyzed, which means she can't blink her eyelid and has difficulty chewing. She spent a long time in the hospital and needed eyelid surgery to keep her right eye from drying out. The surgery has been a great success, and she can still see well out of her eye.

Claire is small for her age, but very spirited. She requires a special diet, so we blend all of her favorite foods several times a day and add vitamins and minerals to keep her healthy. When Claire was young, she struggled to learn how to eat grass. After spending time with her friend Jude, though, she learned how to graze. Since then, she has never left his side.

Claire is such a sweet and gentle being. She loves being with her friends, being brushed, and receiving attention. If you stop brushing Claire before she feels ready to be done, she will give you the slowest, gentlest head butt and politely ask you to continue.

Maya

(Photograph on page 98)

We were contacted about a young calf who appeared to be slowly starving to death in a field at their neighbor's farm. For several weeks, they had watched her trying unsuccessfully to eat and getting weaker and weaker, until she could barely stand.

The farmer agreed to surrender this calf, whom we named Maya, and we rushed to pick her up and take her to the hospital. The veterinarian discovered lots of decaying hay stuck in the back of her throat. She was so malnourished, she couldn't swallow.

The veterinarians determined Maya had a form of "muscle wasting" that prevented normal physical development. It took time to develop a food regimen that she would adhere to consistently, and which gave her all the nutrients she needed to grow healthy. Maya had to return to the hospital several times during this period for intravenous nutrients. On her second to last visit, her medical team said that if she needed further hospitalization, it might be time to euthanize her instead. We brought her home, and she started to finally do a little better.

After a few weeks, she started to decline again. We called the hospital and begged for them to take her back and help her one more time; thankfully, they agreed. That was the last time Maya ever needed hospitalization! She has been doing great ever since.

Maya is tiny for her age and breed. She still suffers from nutrient deficiencies. We make her vitamin smoothies every day, which seem to have saved her life.

Maya is quite rambunctious and opinionated! For a little girl, she has a big, deep bellow that she sounds any time she disagrees with something that is happening! She is bossy and naughty, and we love it. Maya likes to run and play, and she has a sense of adventure. She loves hanging out with her best friends, Jude and Claire, but also takes solo walks around her pastures just for fun.

Best Friends Jude, Claire, and Maya

One of the most beautiful and interesting aspects of sanctuary work is watching the animals develop relationships with one another. We have seen many wonderful friendships form, but none more so than the friendship between Jude, Claire, and Maya.

These three really resonated with each other from the instant they met. One of the most memorable days here at Lancaster Farm Sanctuary was when we introduced baby Claire to Jude. We had been trying and trying to get her to eat grass and hay. We hand-picked bowls of the lushest blades we could find, yet she was resistant to eating—until she met Jude. Claire watched Jude grazing. Jude, with his cleft lip and his wild tongue shooting out the sides, was scooping up grass and eating it out of the corner of his crooked mouth. And then it was as if Claire said to herself, “Oh, I can do that too!” Within minutes, she started eating happily alongside him! They have been inseparable ever since.

Maya came along a few months later, and it was so obvious she belonged with them. She takes great comfort in being by Jude’s side. We say that both Claire and Maya refer to him as “Momma Jude.” He is much larger than both girls, and they love to lie near him, rest their heads on him, and have adventures with him around the sanctuary.

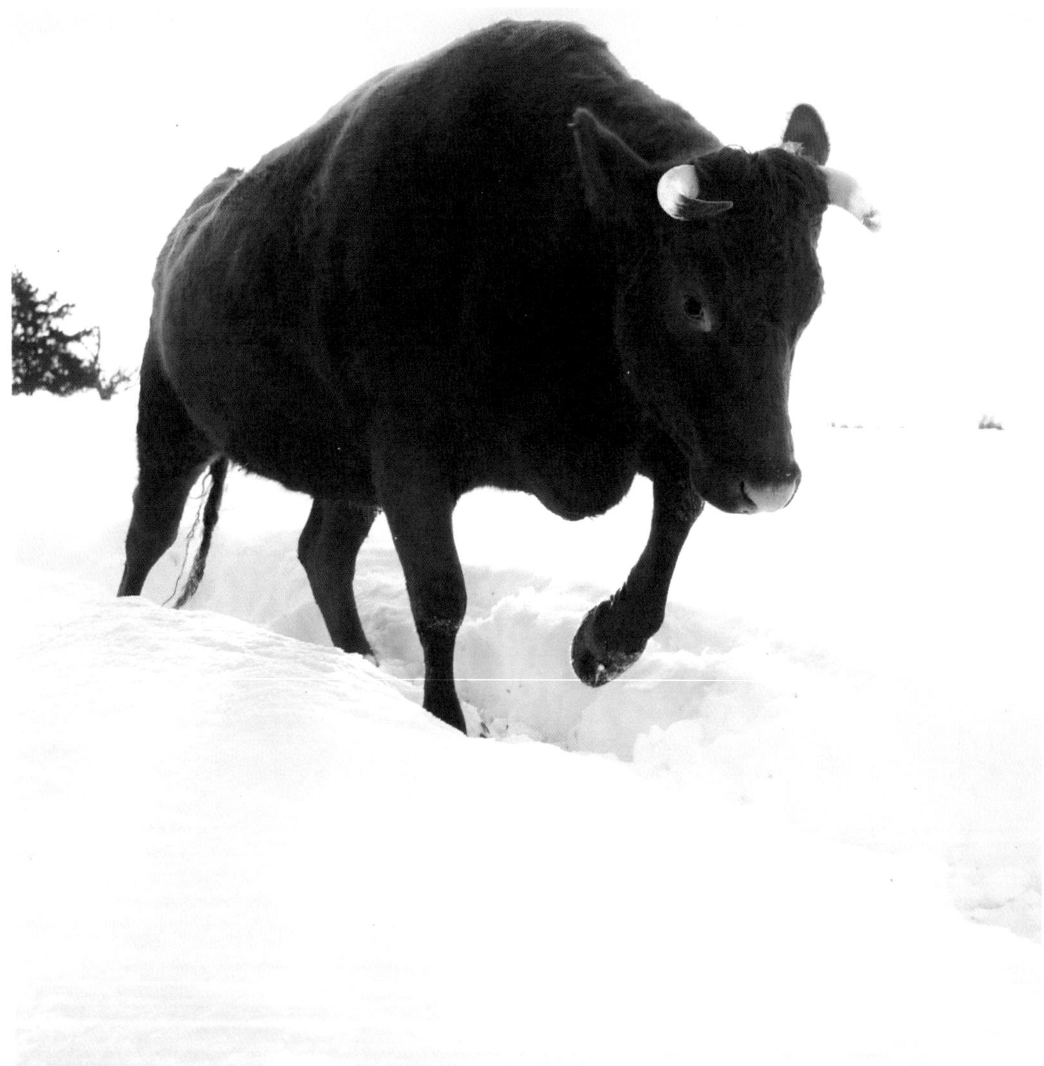

Aggie *(Red Shorthorn)*

As a tiny one-month-old calf, Aggie likely escaped from a livestock auction, as she appeared at a home about a mile away on the sale day. She seems to have followed the railroad tracks to a farmhouse, where a kind woman found her and arranged for her to be taken to a sanctuary.

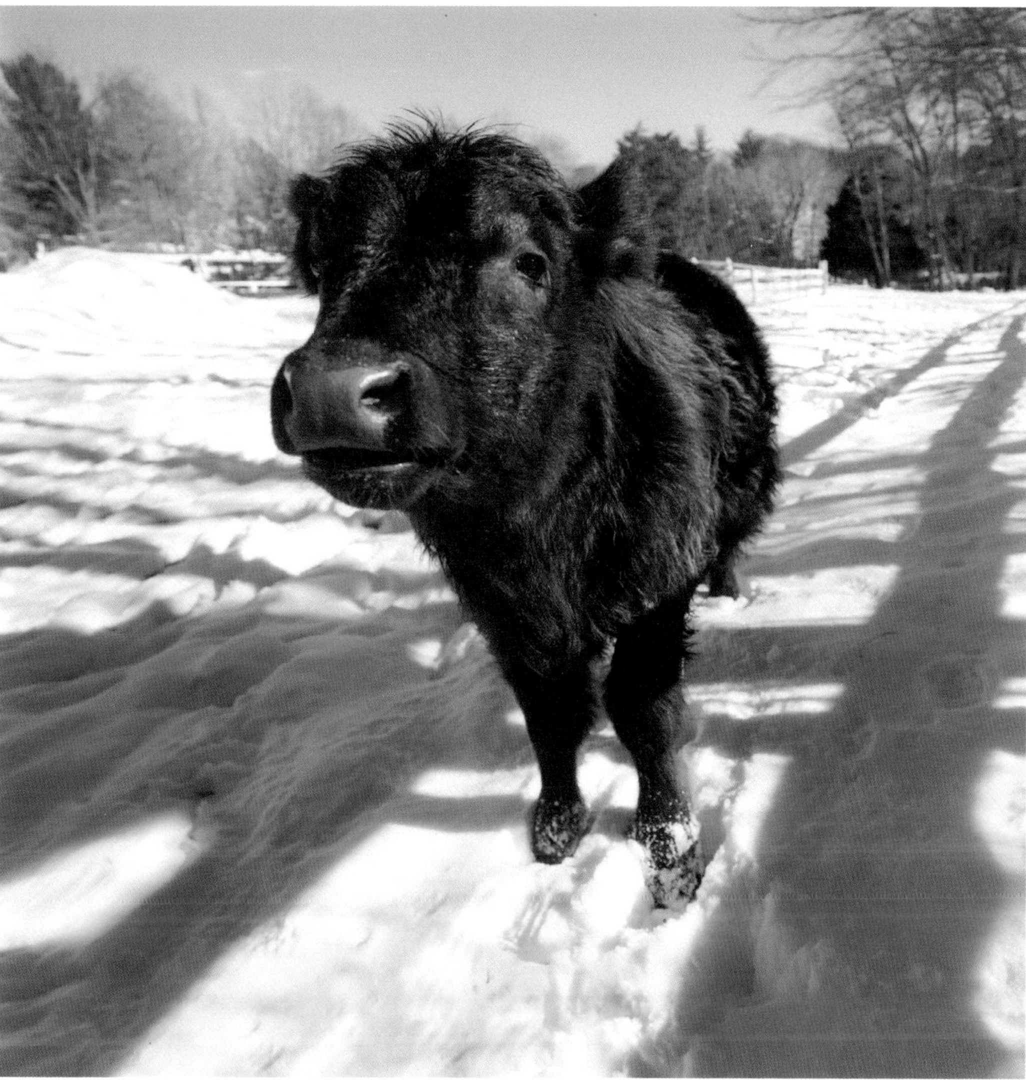

Wilbur *(Hereford/Angus mix)*

After a strenuous and problematic labor, Wilbur's mother died on the small farm where he was born. Wilbur was alone. The farmer bottle-fed him. But a few days later, a loose dog attacked Wilbur and bit his leg, resulting in a deep, infected wound. Eventually, the farmer asked a sanctuary to give him a good life.

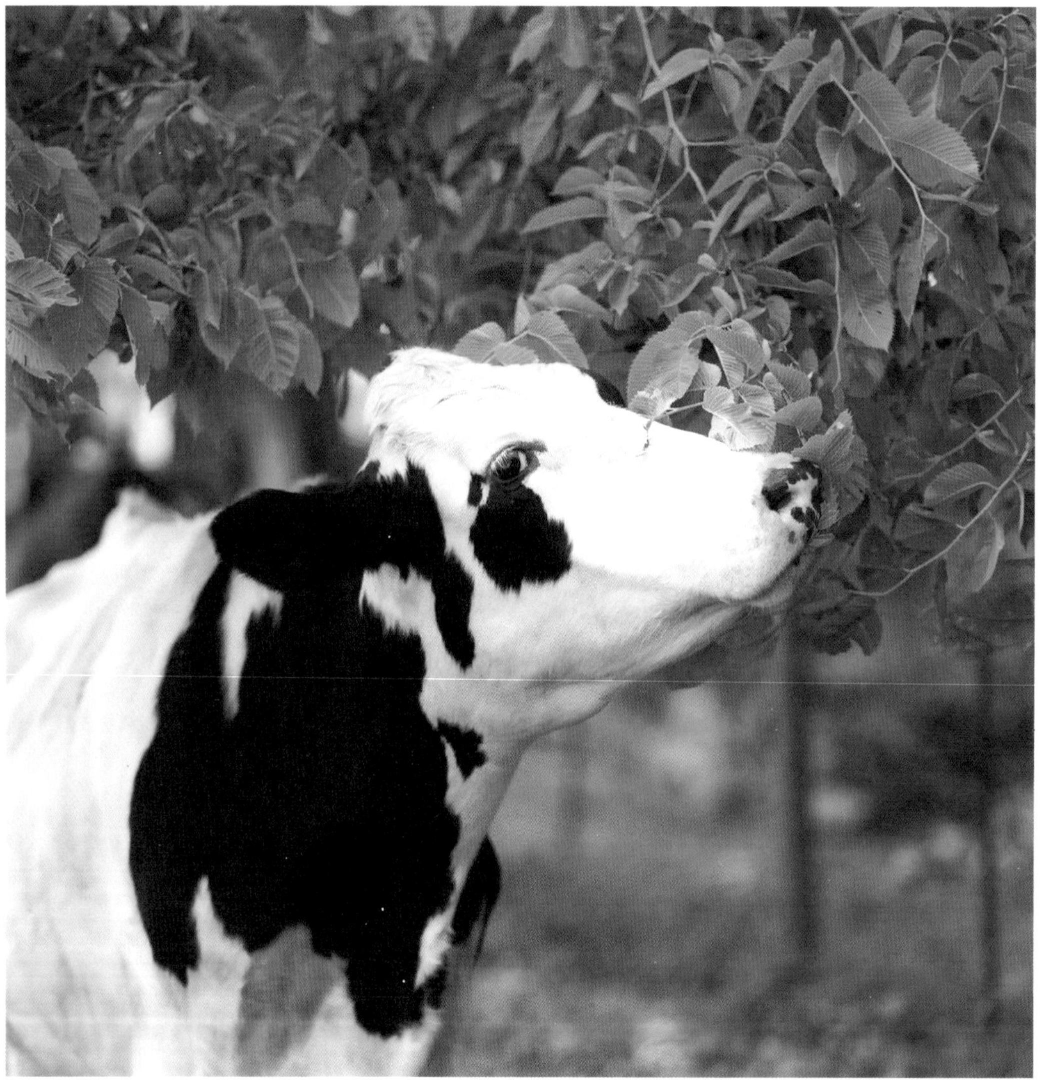

***Owen** (Holstein)*
As calves, Owen and his best friend, Matteo, were rescued from the same dairy farm. When he was young, Owen delighted in rolling his favorite blue ball around the pasture.

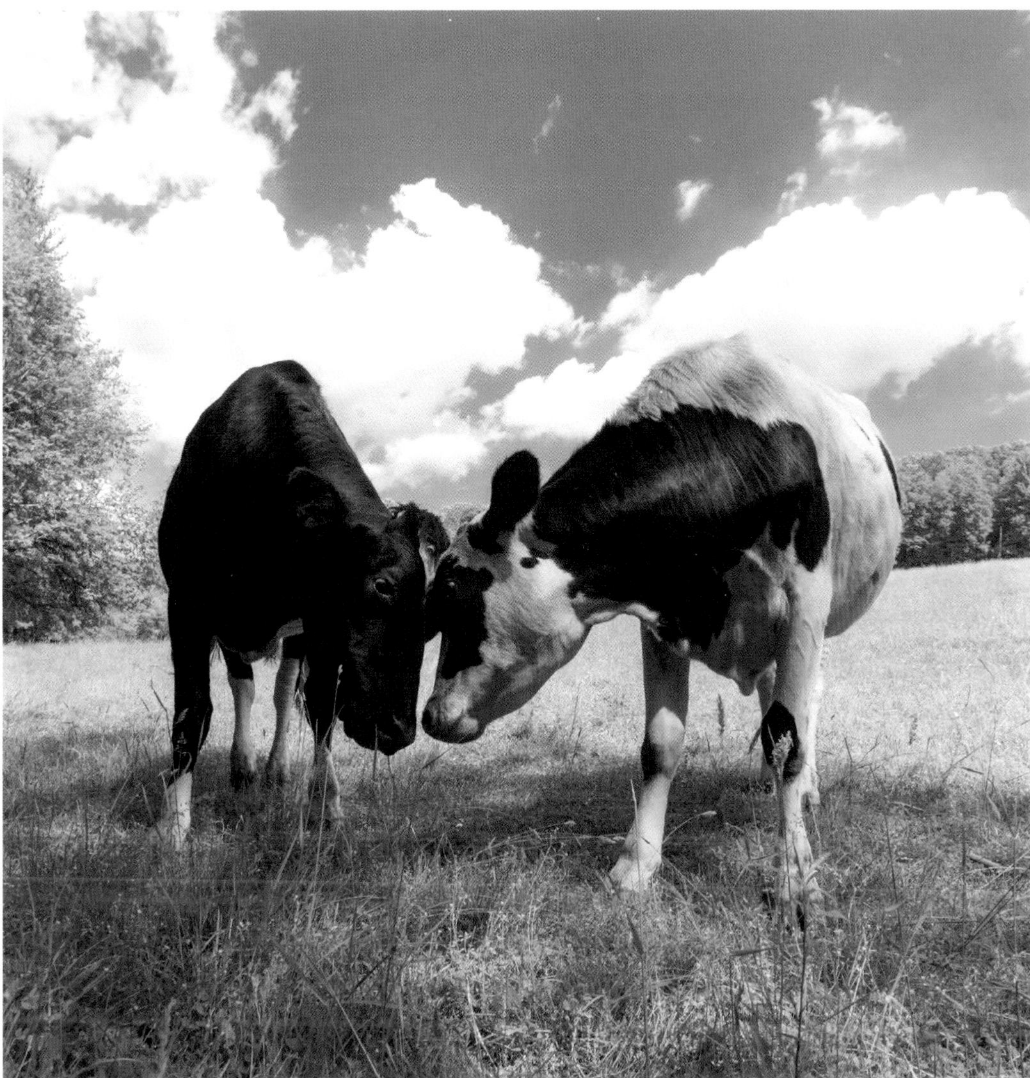

Matteo *(Holstein) and* ***Owen***

Growing up together in a herd, these steers have formed a strong friendship. They share their days together, and often snuggle close as they drift off to sleep at night in their barn.

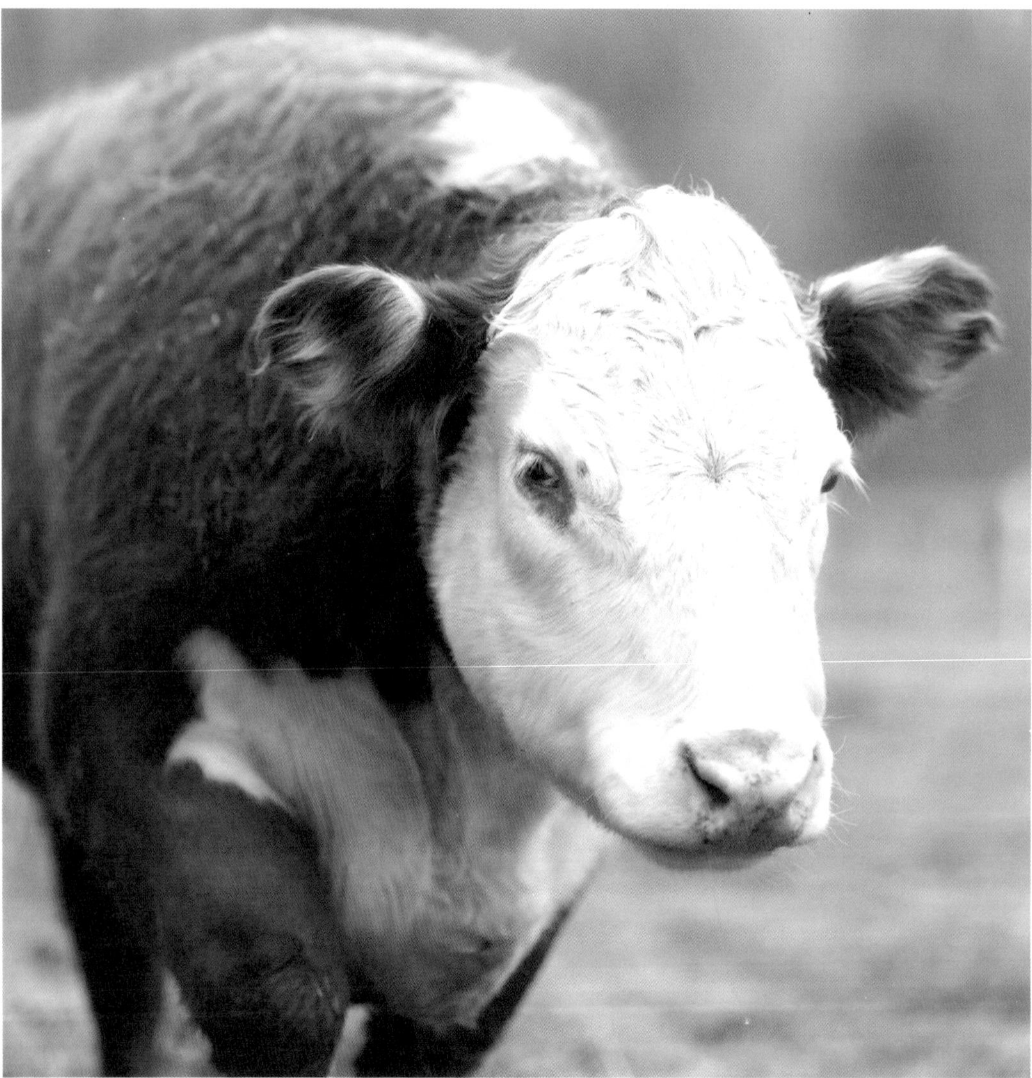

***Carmen** (Hereford)*

Carmen was born on a small beef cattle farm where, as a small calf, sepsis from a bad illness led to vision loss. See "Sweet Carmen" on page 23.

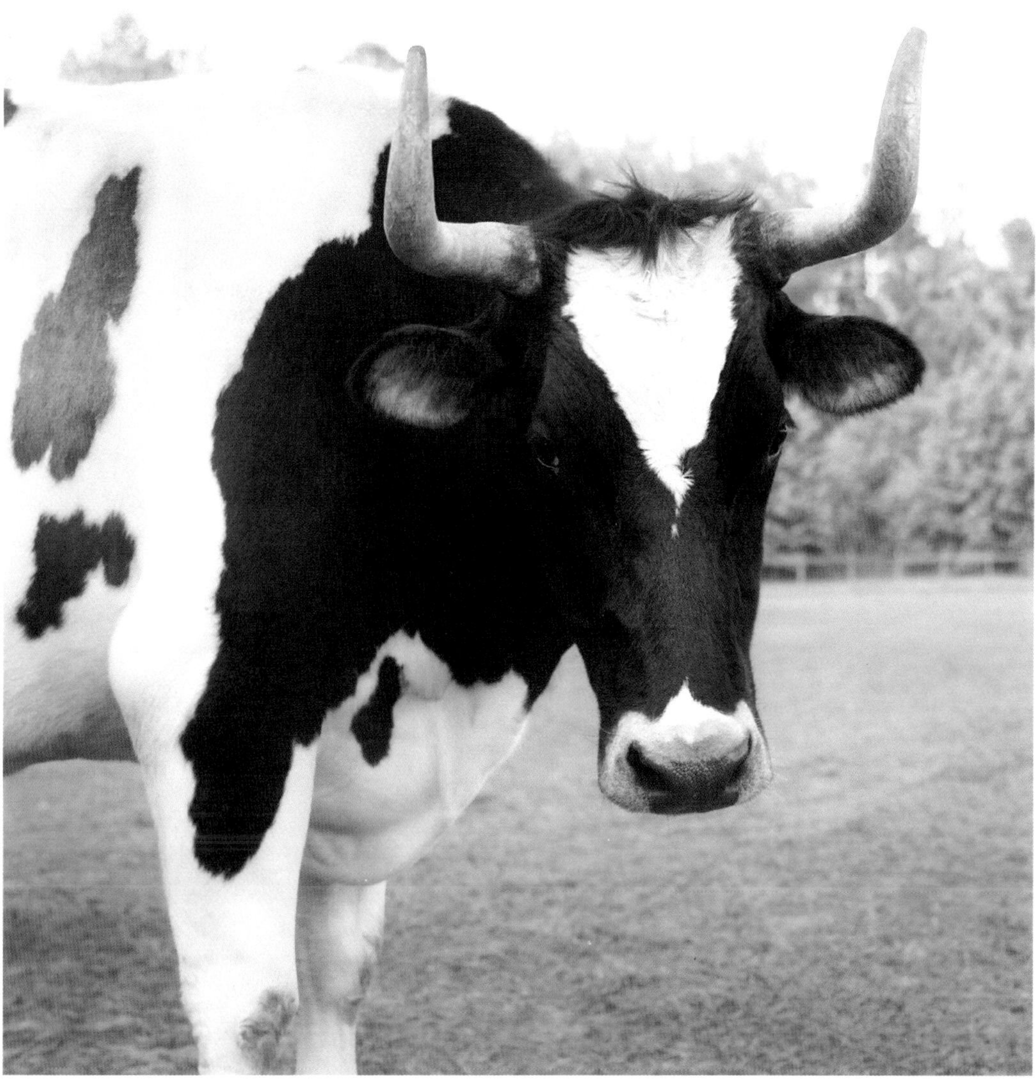

George Harrison Valentino *(Holstein mix)*

George Harrison Valentino would have spent his first weeks of life alone in a pen, to be slaughtered for veal, but he was so cute and friendly that a university student rescued him. He was hand-raised by kind people, but as he grew, he started to break out of his pasture to look for other cows. He was evidently lonely for members of his own kind. In sanctuary, he has a large herd of friends.

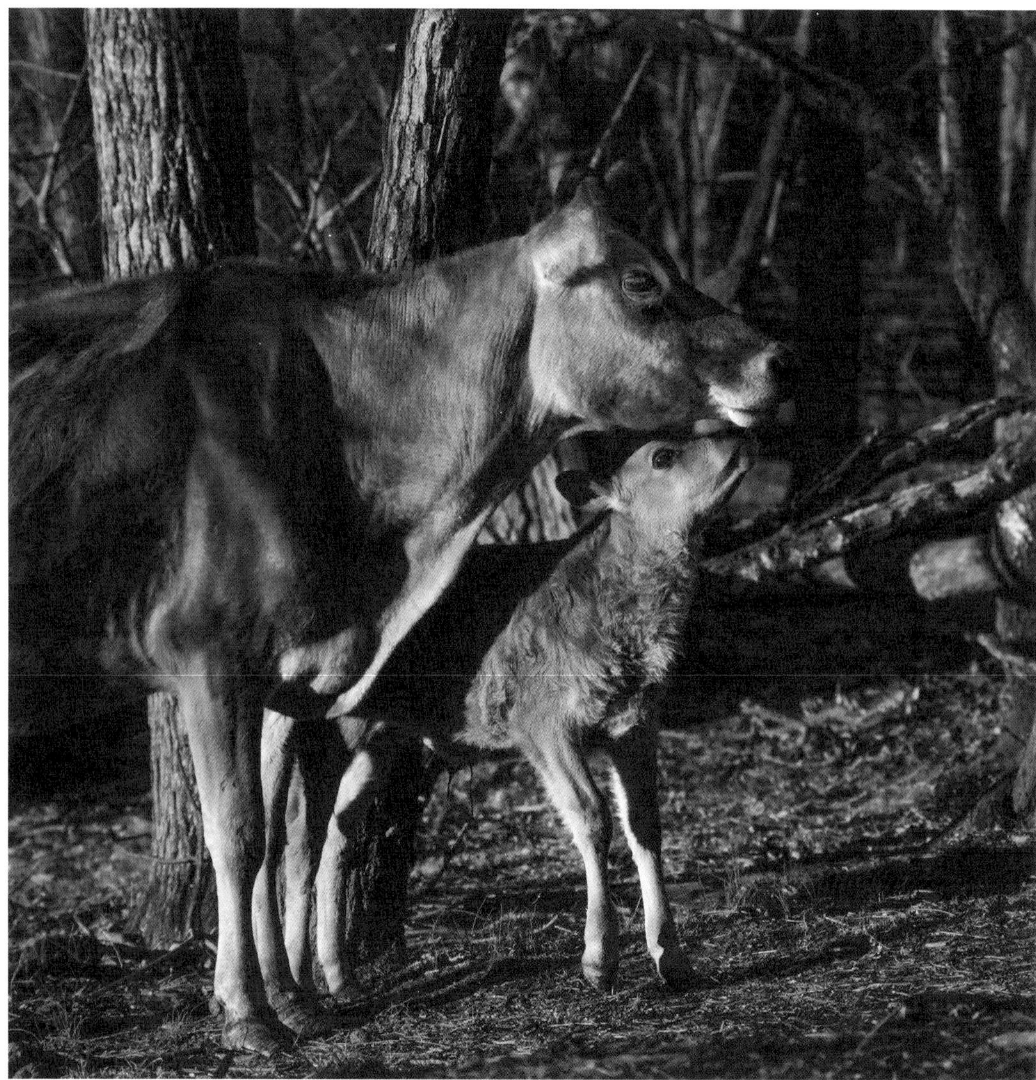

***Maple** (Jersey) and **Grayson** (Jersey)*

Photographed in 2019. After seven years as a dairy cow on an Amish farm, Maple was regarded as old and tired. The farmer planned to kill Maple for meat, but agreed to relinquish her instead. She arrived in a sanctuary pregnant with Grayson. *See "Maple and Grayson" on page 125.*

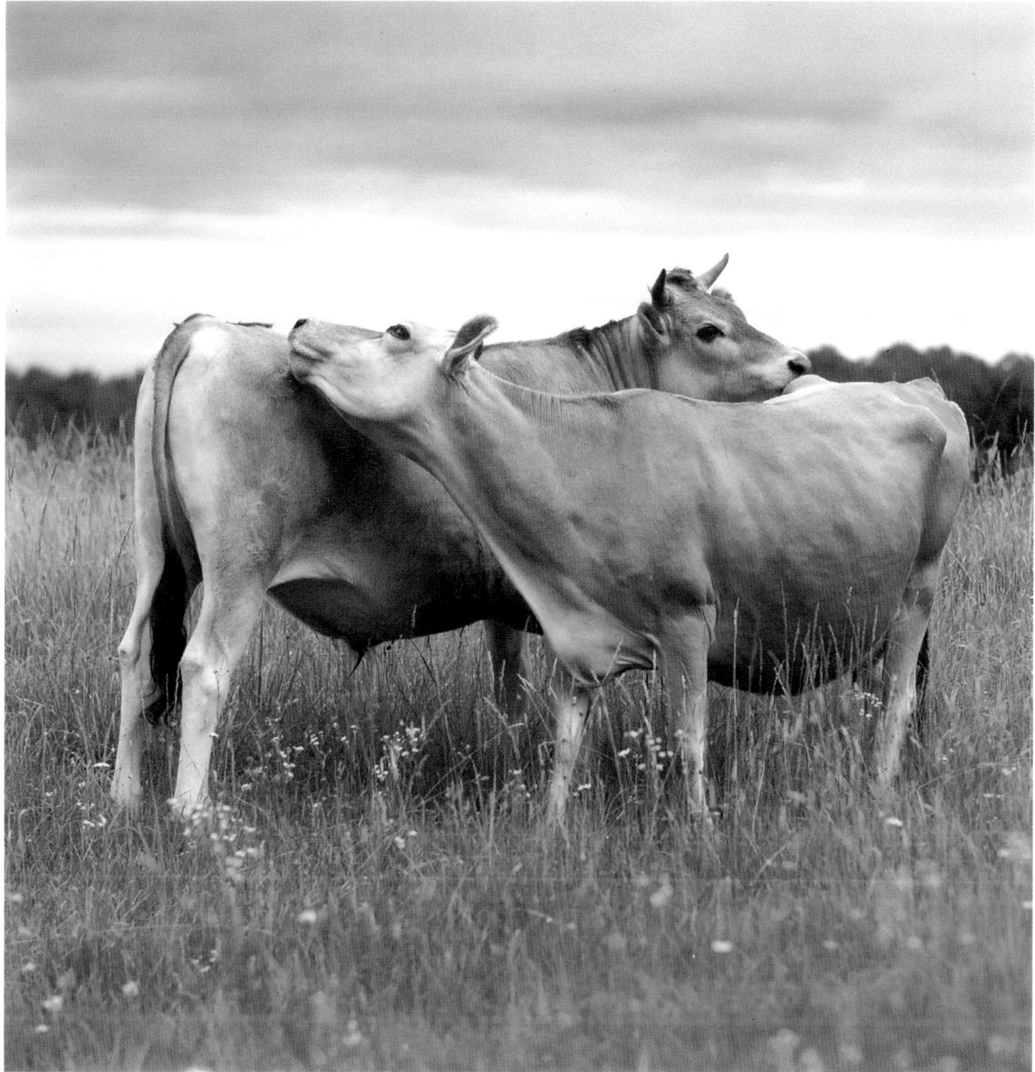

Maple** and **Grayson

Photographed in 2020. Grayson nursed from his mother, Maple, for more than four years. Calves often nurse from their mothers long after they've weaned themselves from her milk, to reinforce their reciprocal bond. Maple very patiently accommodated him, even though he towers over her and sports large, pointy horns.

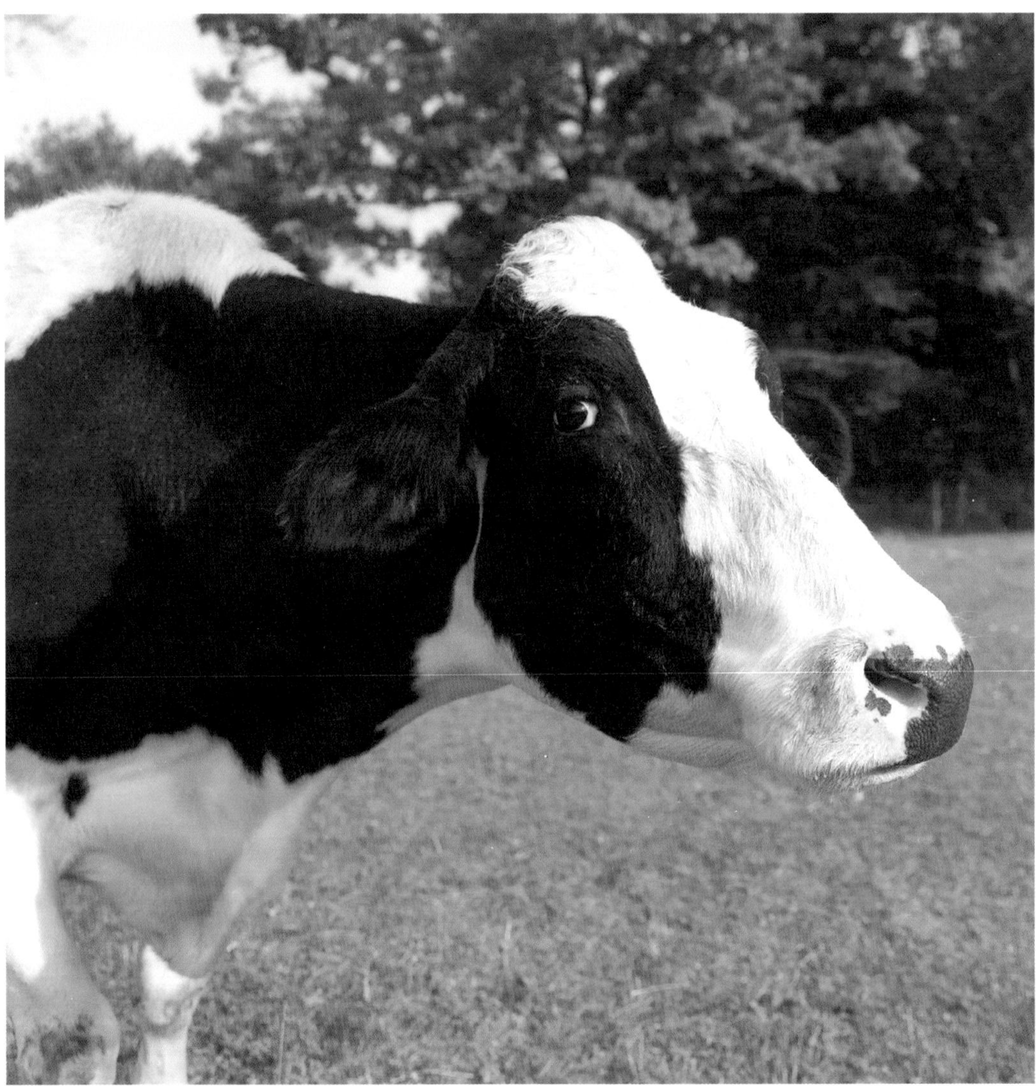

Watson *(Holstein)*

Watson was rescued from a dairy farm as a calf. After living with a foster family for several years, he found his permanent home in a sanctuary. *See "Watson" on page 101.*

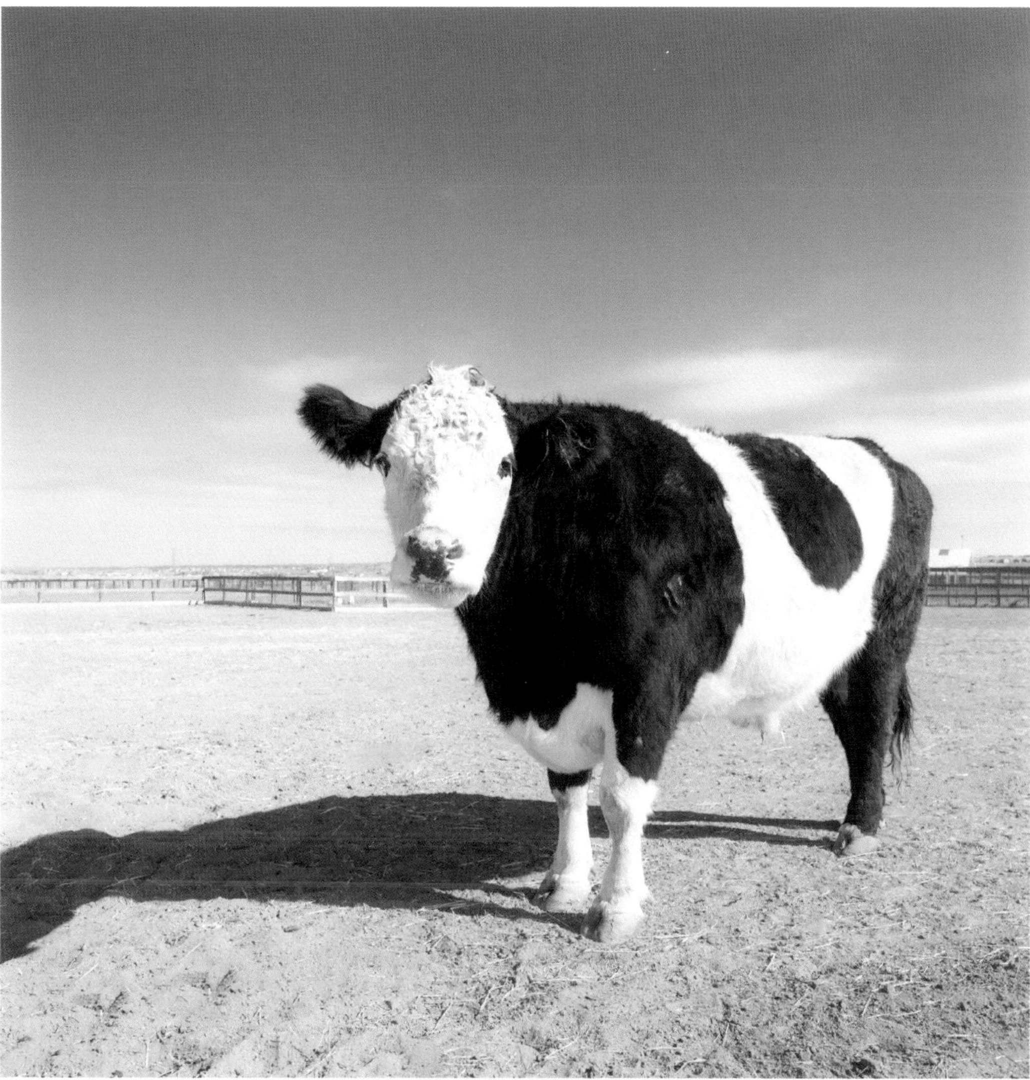

***Milo** (Hereford)*

Over 1,000 animals lived in horrific conditions, surrounded by decaying carcasses and barbed wire. The American Society for the Prevention of Cruelty to Animals (ASPCA) rescued Milo and two other cows.

Milo loves butt and tail scratches and does a little dance every time he receives them.

ROSIE'S FARM SANCTUARY

by Michele Waldman, Founder and President
Potomac, Maryland

Mickey and Moose

(Photographs on pages 110 and 111)

When you see Mickey and Moose grazing and exploring their pasture together, or sharing a snooze, it is hard to believe there was a time when these two didn't know each other. They are practically attached at the hip. Or, well, at the hoof.

Mickey was born on a dairy farm in Vermont. We had been in conversation with the owner to try to rescue one of their calves. Most, if not all, of their male calves are sent to auction for veal farms. We were incredibly grateful that the farmer agreed to let us have Mickey. We were even allowed to be there at his birth. He was adorable when he was born—a calf version of Bambi the cartoon Disney deer, with skinny legs, fluffy ears, and big brown eyes.

Mickey's mother had no name on the dairy farm, only a number: twenty-two. She was their oldest and most lucrative cow, and had given birth multiple times before, yielding the dairy with not only a significant amount of milk to sell but also many babies to dispose of after birth. To produce milk, a mother cow must be pregnant and give birth. The dairy farms generally auction off or kill the male calves. Mother cows have strong maternal instincts and form close bonds with their babies, and they cry out in distress, sometimes for days, when their calves are taken within hours of being born.

Because Mickey's mom was old, the dairy farmer said we could also have her once she finished lactating, in approximately a year. The natural lifespan of cows is fifteen to twenty years of age, and sometimes even older, but the majority of cows on dairy farms only live until they are about five years old, when their milk production drops, and they are sent to slaughter. Number twenty-two was nine years old, which is considered ancient for cows used on dairy farms. Her body was tired, and her bones fragile, after being continually impregnated her entire adult life.

We were excited to bring number twenty-two to Rosie's Farm Sanctuary to reunite with her son and live the remainder of her life protected and loved. We named her Maggie May, and the countdown was on until we could pick her up and bring her home with us.

In the meantime, we knew that we needed another calf to keep Mickey company. There is no shortage of newborn calves at dairies, but it isn't easy to find farmers who are willing to allow activists to take their calves, even if they have no use for them.

Luckily, we were able to find another dairy farmer in Vermont who agreed to let us take one of their calves. Moose was born only a few days after Mickey. When we picked him up, he was tied to a rope in a dark barn and all alone, without his mother. He had a rough start to life, but Moose was one of the lucky ones. When he was five days old, we were able to liberate him from the dairy farm. He weighed about fifty pounds and was vulnerable and timid.

We introduced Mickey and Moose to each other in the back of our SUV, on the drive from Vermont to our sanctuary in Potomac, Maryland. It was brotherly love at first sight! They immediately smelled and licked each other. They lay side by side for the long drive to their new life at Rosie's, about to start their best adventures.

We were so excited when Mickey and Moose arrived. They were so gangly and awkward. They were happy to be out of the SUV and ran around their new barn, clumsily kicking up their back legs with glee.

After a few days, though, it became evident that Moose was really sick. He had salmonella and an umbilical cord infection from being left on the filthy concrete floor as a newborn. He had to be hospitalized for close to a week. We sent Mickey to the hospital with Moose to keep him company. With medical attention and care, Moose recovered and has been healthy since.

At their new home with us, Mickey and Moose made friends with the other residents of Rosie's Farm Sanctuary—from our furred, feathered and hooved friends to all the humans that welcomed them with love and compassion.

One month before we were to take in Maggie May, Mickey's mom, we found out that she had slipped on a wet dairy floor and hurt her leg. The farmer made the decision to euthanize her, rather than giving us the opportunity to take her to a hospital. We were devastated. In her honor, we named our next rescue, a new mother sheep, after her. Maggie May now lives with us with her two baby sheep, Machu and Picchu.

Fast forward to today, Mickey and Moose are still living the good life. They're like the Brad Pitt and George Clooney of the animal kingdom—charming, handsome and always ready for a snuggle. Sure, they might be a tad bigger than your average lap dog, but that doesn't stop them from trying to climb into your lap for cuddles. They have no clue as to how big they are. They are currently over 1,000 pounds each but will likely grow to 1,500 pounds. These boys remain popular residents amongst the staff and visitors today.

There are over nine million cows used for dairy in the United States alone right now. Each one of these mothers has given birth to a baby like Mickey and Moose. These babies are considered "waste products" of the dairy industry; they are killed before they even get the chance to run in a pasture or feel the warmth of the sun. Mickey and Moose may not have known their mothers, but they will only know love and kindness for the rest of their days, which makes them some of the most fortunate bovines in the world.

Rosie's is situated in a residential neighborhood in Potomac, Maryland, just outside of Washington, D.C. This prime, highly accessible location was specifically chosen so that more people could visit easily to tour and volunteer, as well as to be in the hotbed of other animal welfare organizations for collaborative legislative and policy action.

We opened in early 2022, leveraging the ripple effect of change through connections and community. Because of our well-populated location, we enable thousands of people, of all ages, each year to connect with our animal ambassadors and learn about compassionate living.

We rescue, rehabilitate, and provide forever homes to animals abused across all parts of the industrial animal agriculture system, who serve as ambassadors of their kind. Our animal ambassadors include not only Mickey and Moose, but also farmed pigs, potbelly pigs, horses, goats, sheep, and hens. Our small size allows for meaningful interactions and connections between our visitors and our animal ambassadors.

So, if you ever find yourself near Washington, D.C., be sure to swing by Rosie's Farm Sanctuary for a dose of animal antics and a whole lot of heart. Who knows? You might just leave with a newfound appreciation for the furry, feathered, and hoofed friends who call this place home.

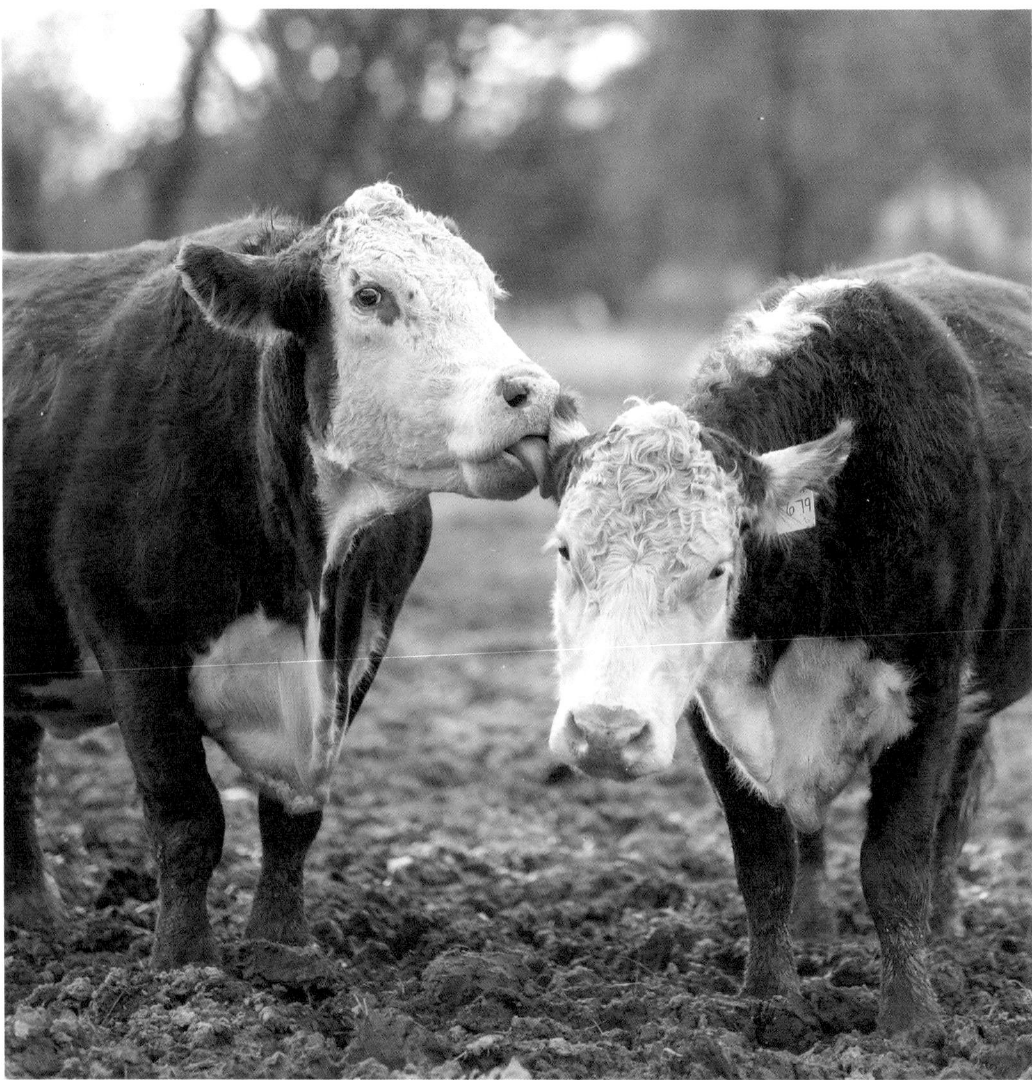

Siena *(Hereford) and* ***Tawny*** *(Hereford)*

When a farm near Philadelphia, Pennsylvania, closed, Siena and Tawny were saved from being sent to auction along with several other animals.

Both cows love spending time in the stream that runs through their pasture, where they can drink the chill water and cool off.

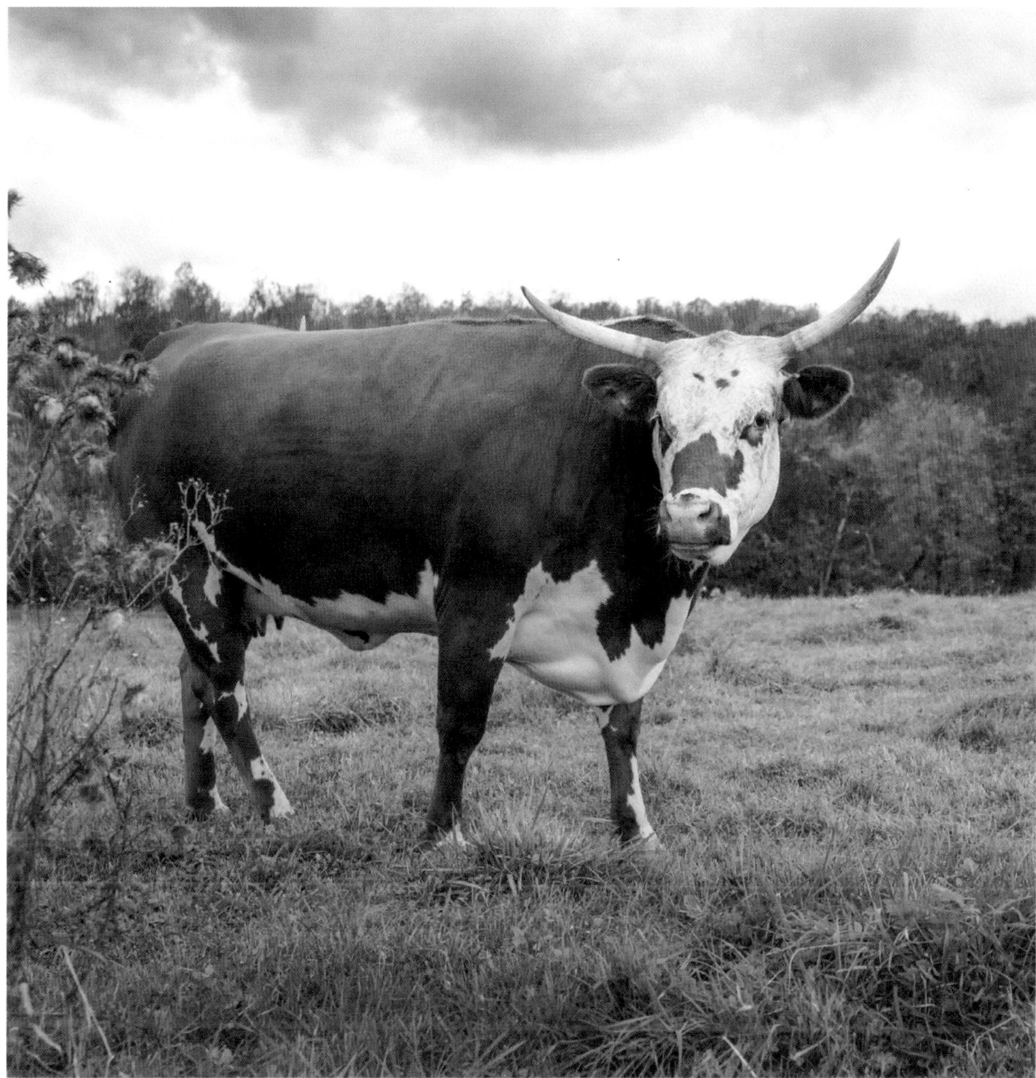

***Gauri** (Breed unknown)*

Gauri's name means "shining" in Sanskrit.

After the legal owner of 300 animals died, the animals were neglected. Gauri was the last to be rescued and now thrives in a sanctuary. Though she enjoys her herd, Gauri cherishes her alone time and is often found at the pasture's edge, watching wildlife or greeting visitors.

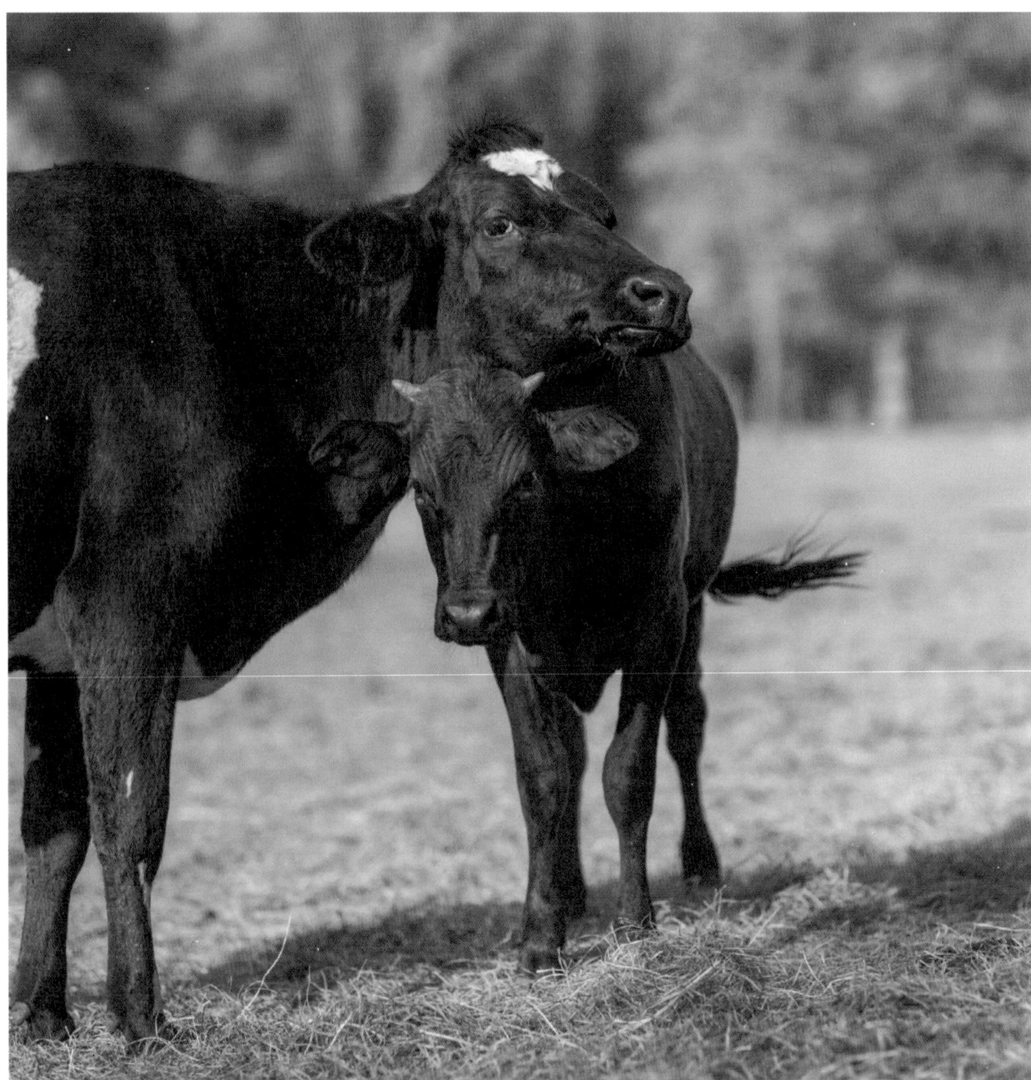

Valentina *(Holstein) and* ***Pablo*** *(Holstein/Zebu)*

A kind couple rescued Valentina and her best friend, another cow named Cinnabun, from a dairy. When the couple's health declined and they could no longer care for the cows, the couple sought a permanent home for these close friends. When Valentina arrived in a sanctuary, she was pregnant with Pablo.

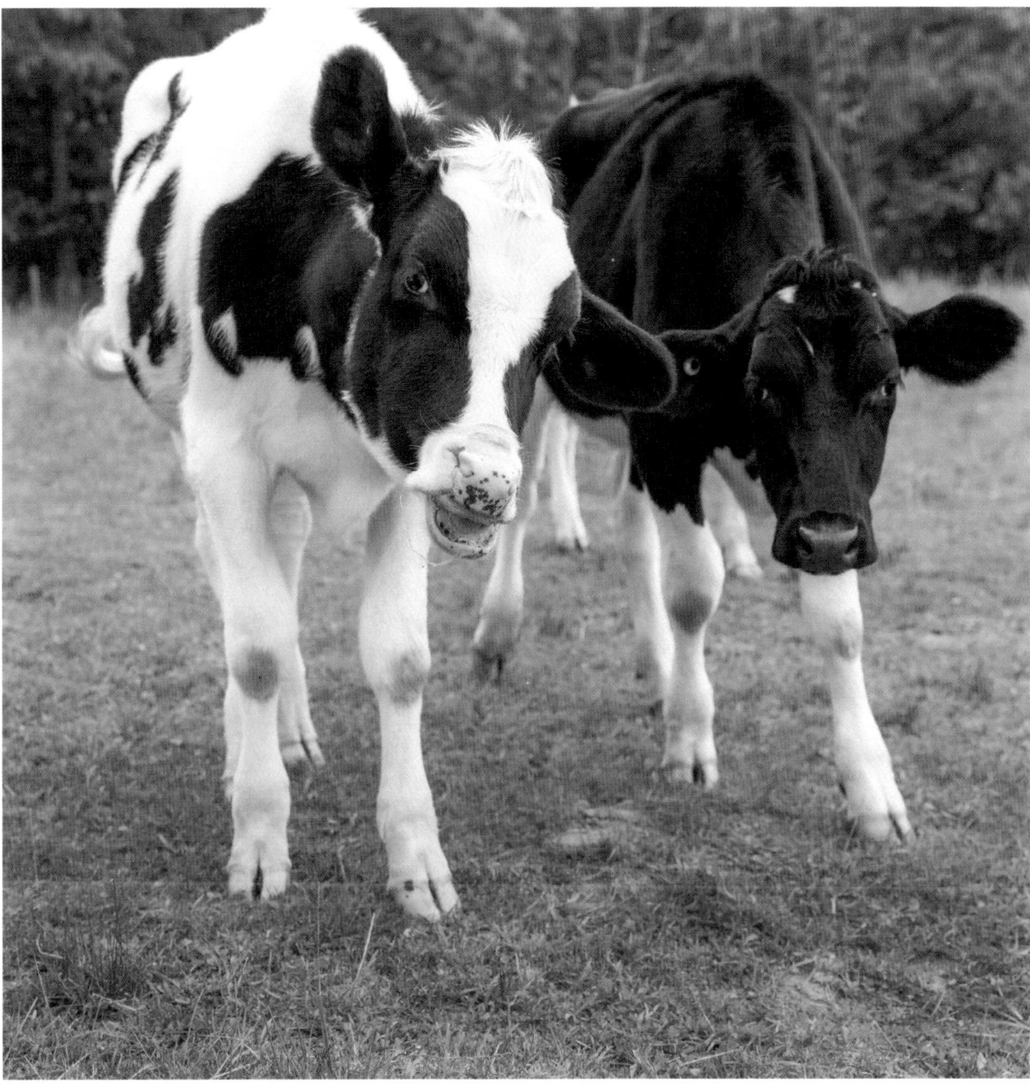

***Jake** (Holstein) and **Marley** (Holstein)*

A Massachusetts dairy farmer relinquished these calves along with two more to a rescue team. Some smaller dairy operations are agreeable to giving their male calves a home. Doing so saves the farmer the trouble of sending them to auction, where common breeds such as Holsteins fetch a relatively small price. Unfortunately, all of the farmed animal sanctuaries in the United States combined can give homes to only a tiny fraction of the millions of male calves born each year.

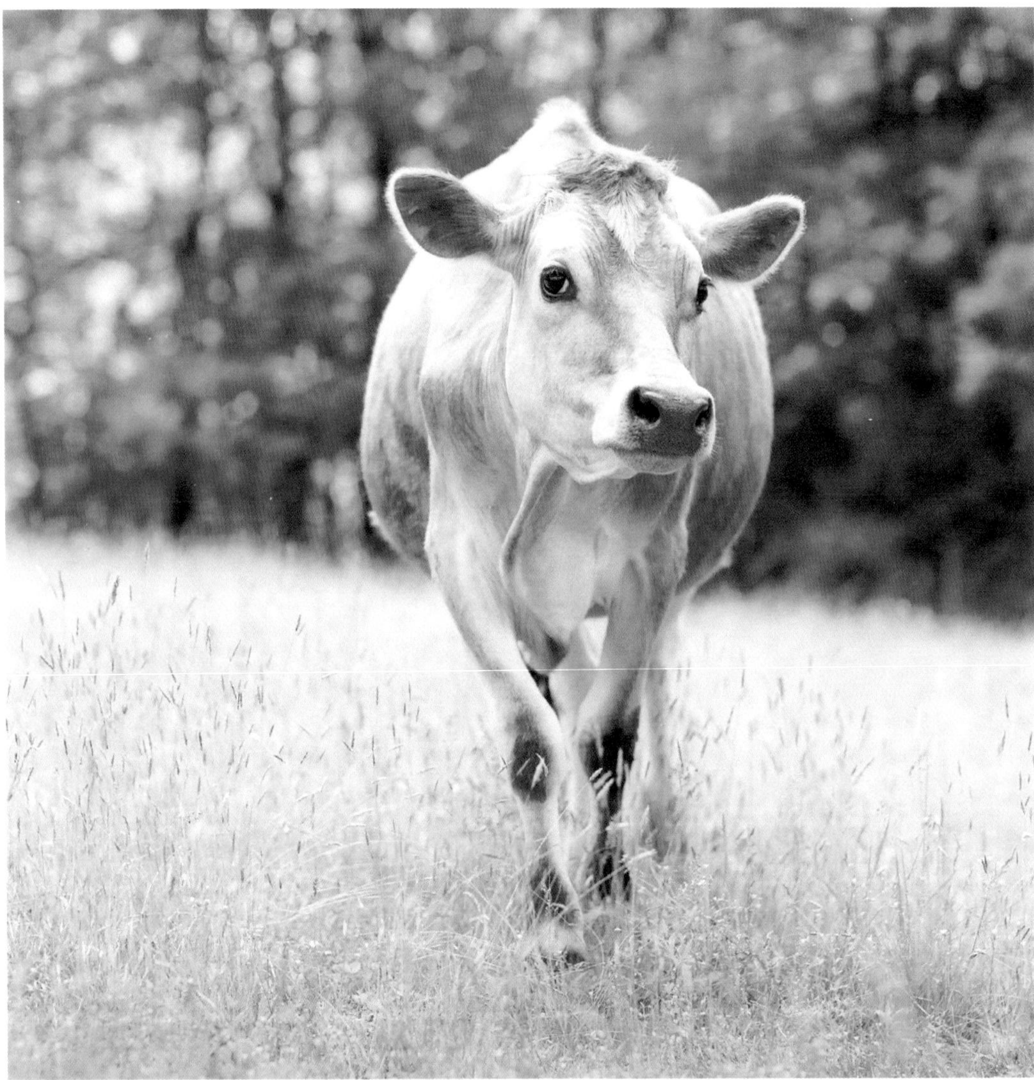

Luke *(Jersey)*

Born on a dairy farm, Luke would have been sent to auction. A young intern at the dairy farm learned about the treatment of male calves and desperately wanted to save this baby. She emailed as many places as she could think of, until she found a sanctuary that had space available and could give Luke a home.

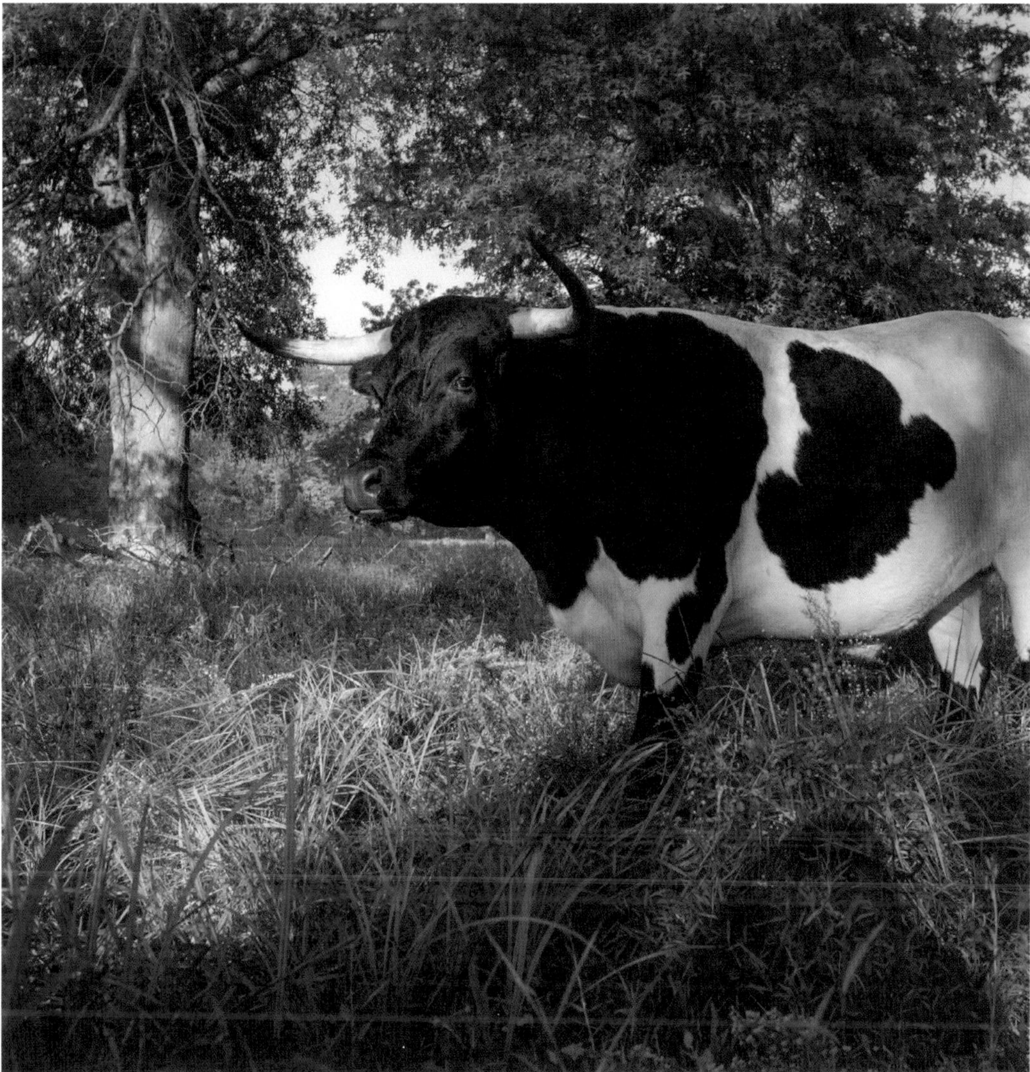

Elliot *(Longhorn)*

Elliot was born in a livestock auction while his mother, Lucy, awaited slaughter. He lay in the kill pen for three days, expected to die. A horse rescuer purchased Lucy and Elliot and took them to a veterinary hospital. The auction house was frigid, and Elliot was very sick when he and Lucy were rescued. After struggling for his life, Elliot grew healthy and strong and was later reunited with his mother in a sanctuary.

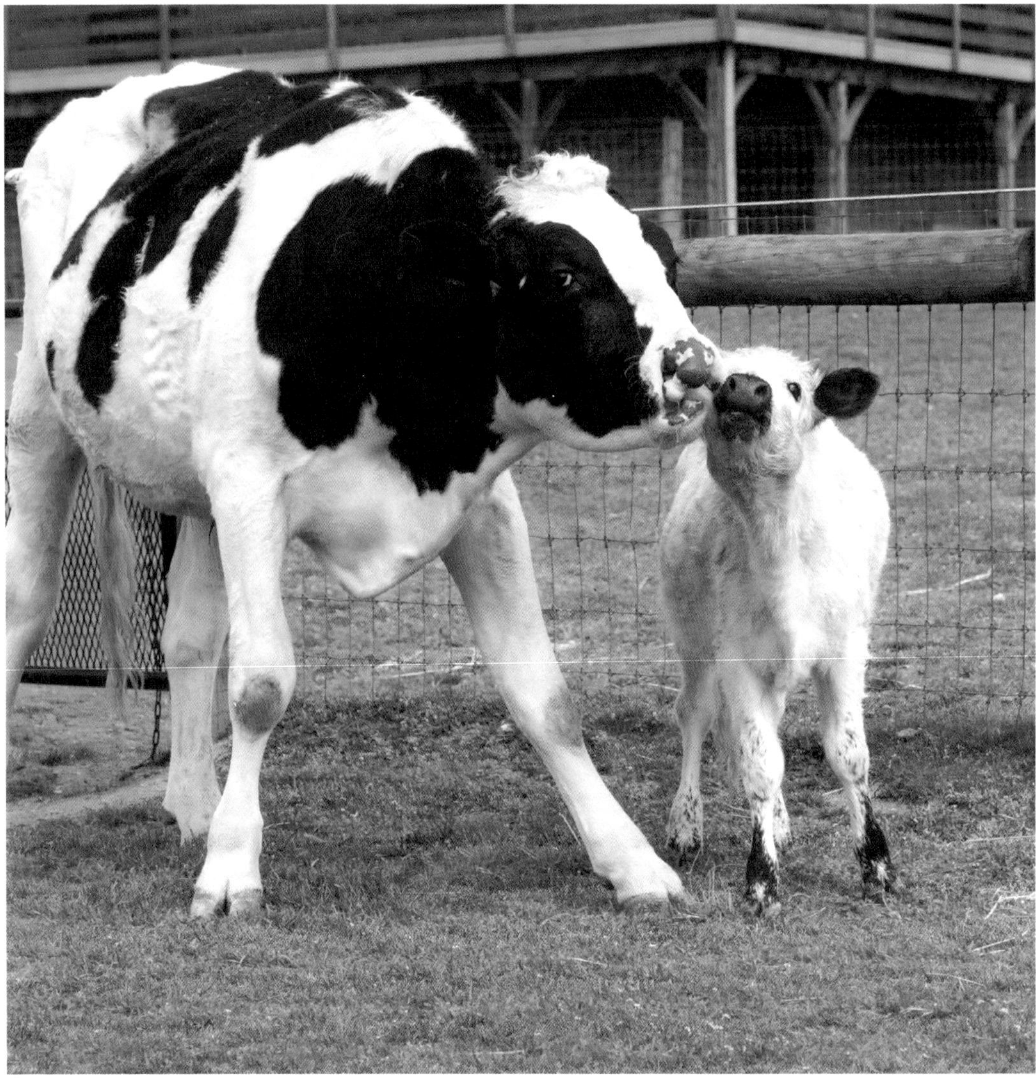

***Jude** (Holstein) and **Maya** (Dexter)*

Jude was born with a cleft palate on a dairy farm. Maya was rescued from starvation on a farm local to a sanctuary.

See "Jude" on page 73 and "Maya" on page 74.

Also see "Best Friends Jude, Claire, and Maya" on page 75.

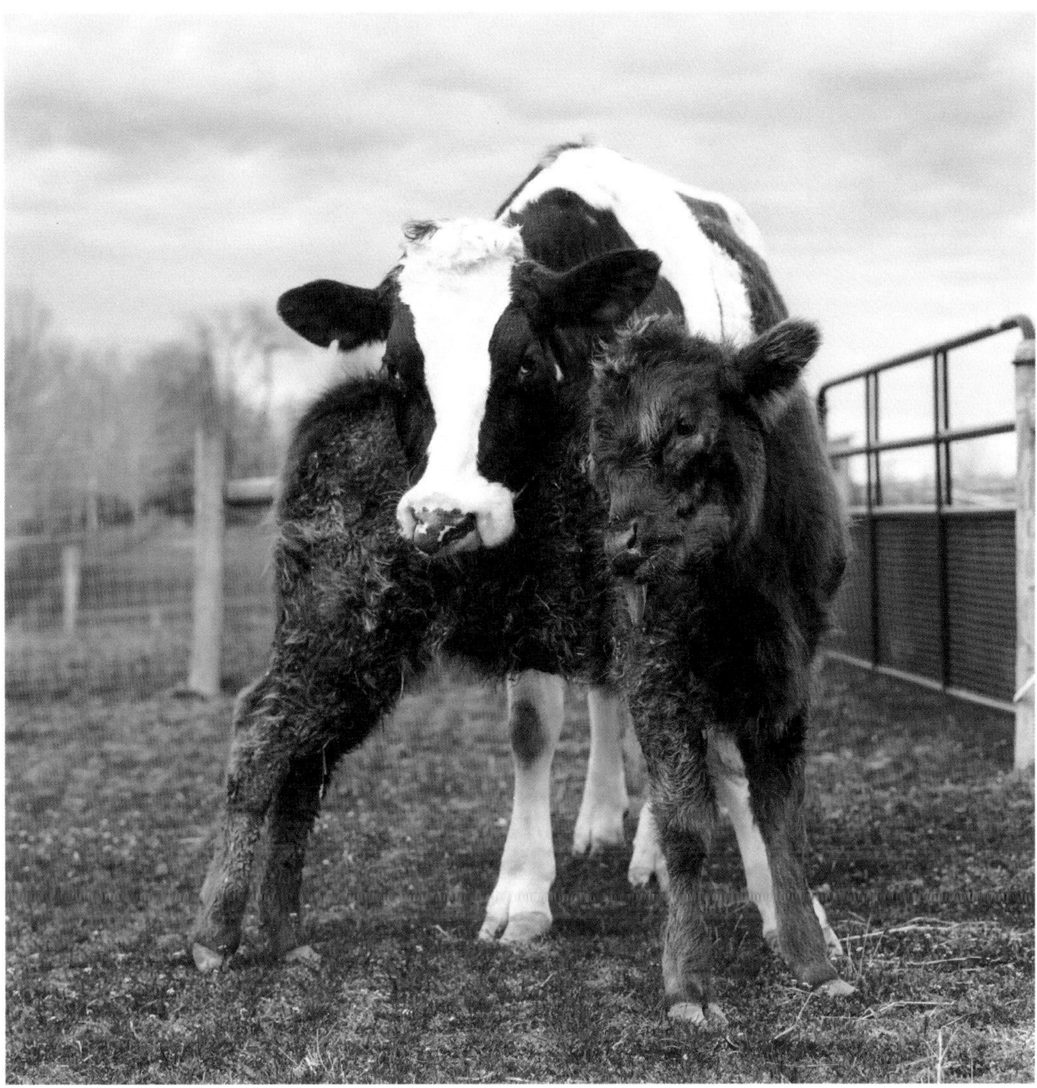

Jude *and* ***Claire*** *(Angus mix)*

Claire was born on a beef farm with a birth defect that left half of her face paralyzed, as well as a corneal ulcer that prevented her from blinking one eye.

See "Claire" on page 74 and "Best Friends Jude, Claire, and Maya" on page 75.

PEACEFUL FIELDS SANCTUARY

By John Netzel, President and Founder
Winchester, Virginia

Watson

(Photograph on page 86)

Watson, a Holstein steer, is seventeen years old. He's over 6' 2" tall at the shoulder and weighs more than 2,500 lbs. Not only is he tall, but his body is also massive like a bodybuilder's. Watson's head alone weighs more than most people! He truly is a gentle giant, and he has many fans. Rescued as a calf from a dairy farm in West Virginia to prevent him from being killed, he now enjoys a leisurely life in his golden years in our sanctuary. He loves to chase after apples, chomp pumpkins, and have the velvet skin around his eyes rubbed.

One year, a large pumpkin patch appeared from seeds out of pumpkins fed to the animals the autumn before. The plants grew and grew, and eventually small green pumpkins appeared. We were amazed how the animals ignored them and left them alone. Finally, the day came when the pumpkins changed color and were ripe. Imagine our astonishment when the very next morning, where the large pumpkin patch had been a perfectly clean area of dirt now lay! Not even a stray leaf fragment could be found. Standing nearby was Watson, and with a burp he seemed to say, "It wasn't me; I have no idea what happened!"

A kiss of gratitude from Watson is like being on a ride at a water amusement park. Welcome to the splash zone! During winter, he smartly spends each day near the hay troughs and water and is amused by the other animals traveling around the property when everything needed is within a few yards of each other. "Silly kids," we imagine he thinks.

Our mission as a vegan farmed animal sanctuary is to provide a safe, loving forever home for farmed animals rescued from cruelty, neglect, or to prevent their death under the guiding Jewish principles of *tikkun olam* (making the world a better place) and *tza'ar ba'alei chayim* (the Jewish mandate to prevent cruelty to animals). Additionally, we educate the community on the problems of animal agriculture and animal cruelty and empower them with actions they can take in their lives to fight animal cruelty, such as adopting a vegan lifestyle.

We've been so honored over the years to develop a bond with Watson and understand his amazing and unique personality. Cows can make great friends!

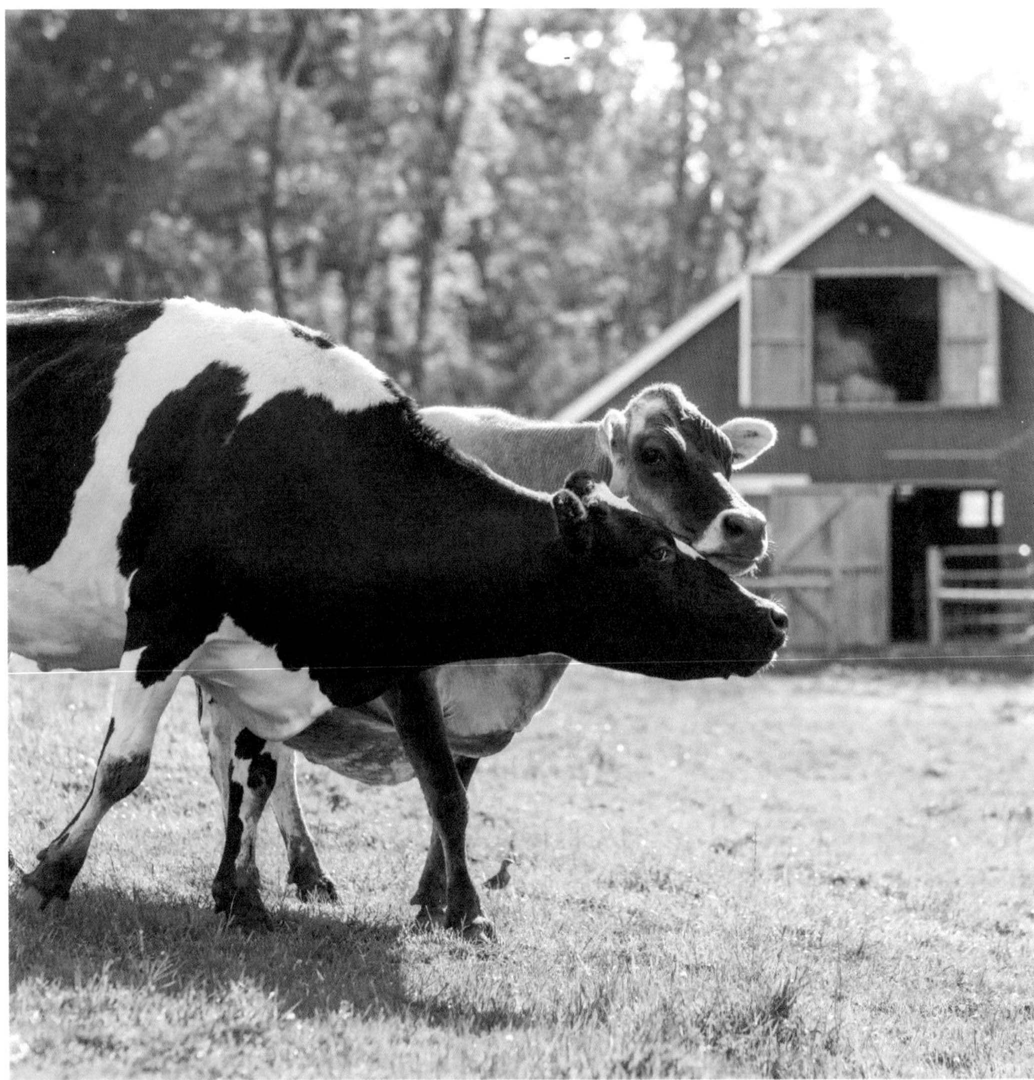

***Ebb** (Jersey mix) and **Flo** (Holstein)*

Ebb suffered a broken pelvis on a dairy farm. After she healed, a veterinarian advised that they stop impregnating her for her safety. Because she was no longer of use to the dairy farm, she was destined for slaughter until she was rescued.

Flo is a dairy farm survivor. An injury to her foot left her with a severe limp. She could no longer be impregnated to produce milk.

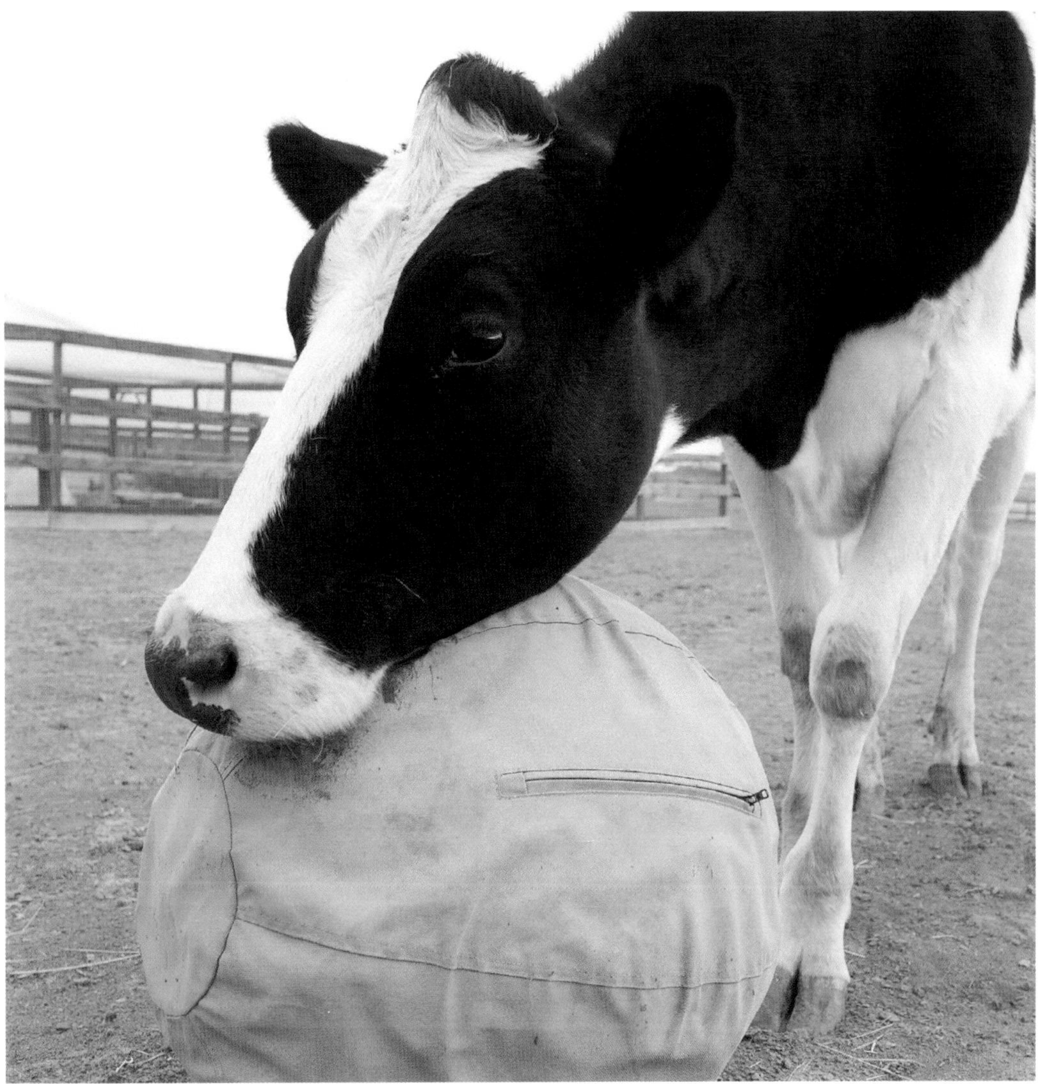

Samantha *(Holstein)*

Born a freemartin on a dairy farm, Samantha would have had no future. See "Samantha" on page 37.

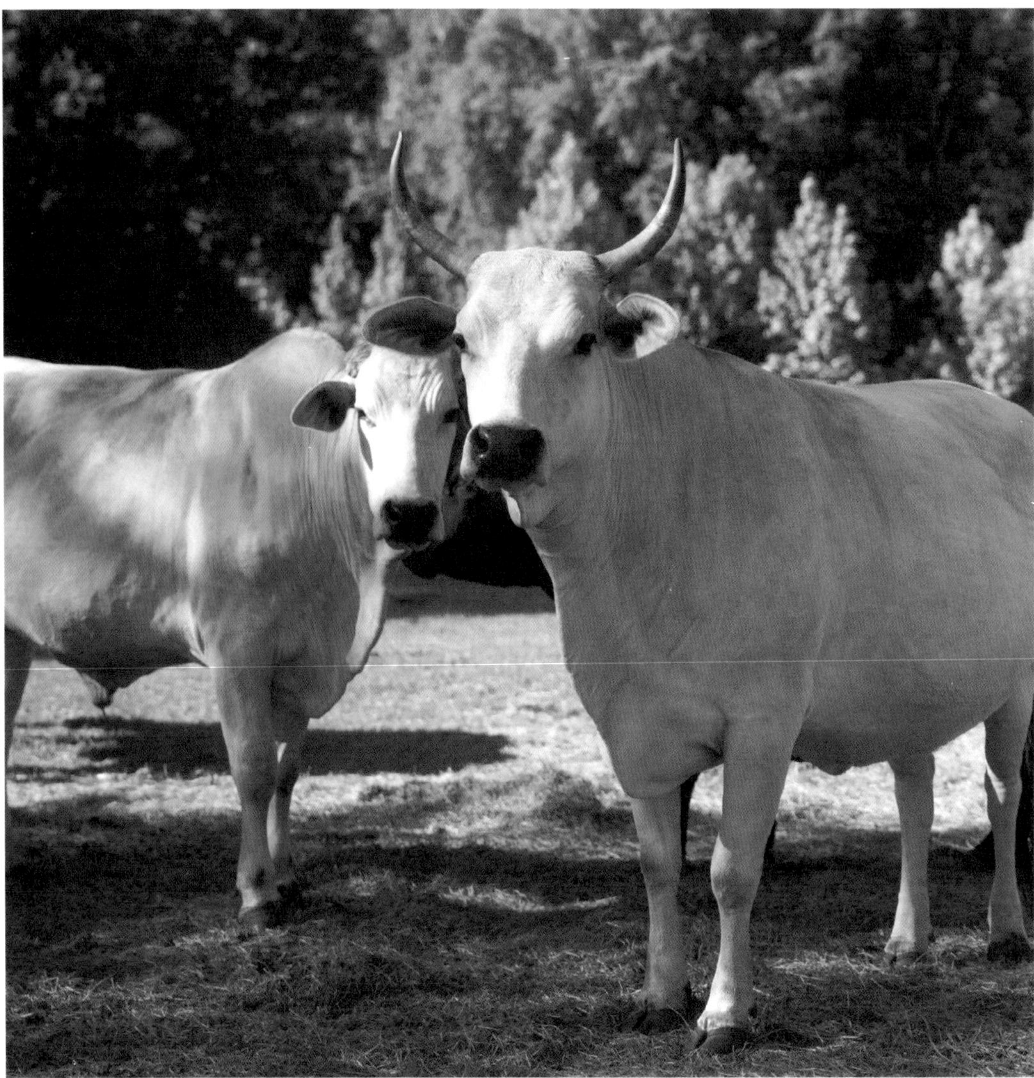

Claire *(Brahman) and* **Ace** *(Brahman)*

Claire was part of the "Feral 12," a group of neglected, starving cows with no contact with humans. They had only a dried-up swamp for water. Rescued and brought to a sanctuary, Claire was already pregnant with Ace.

Claire is the herd matriarch and can often be seen lurking, watching over everyone, making sure no funny business is about. She isn't a fan of human caresses but occasionally comes over for a cow cookie.

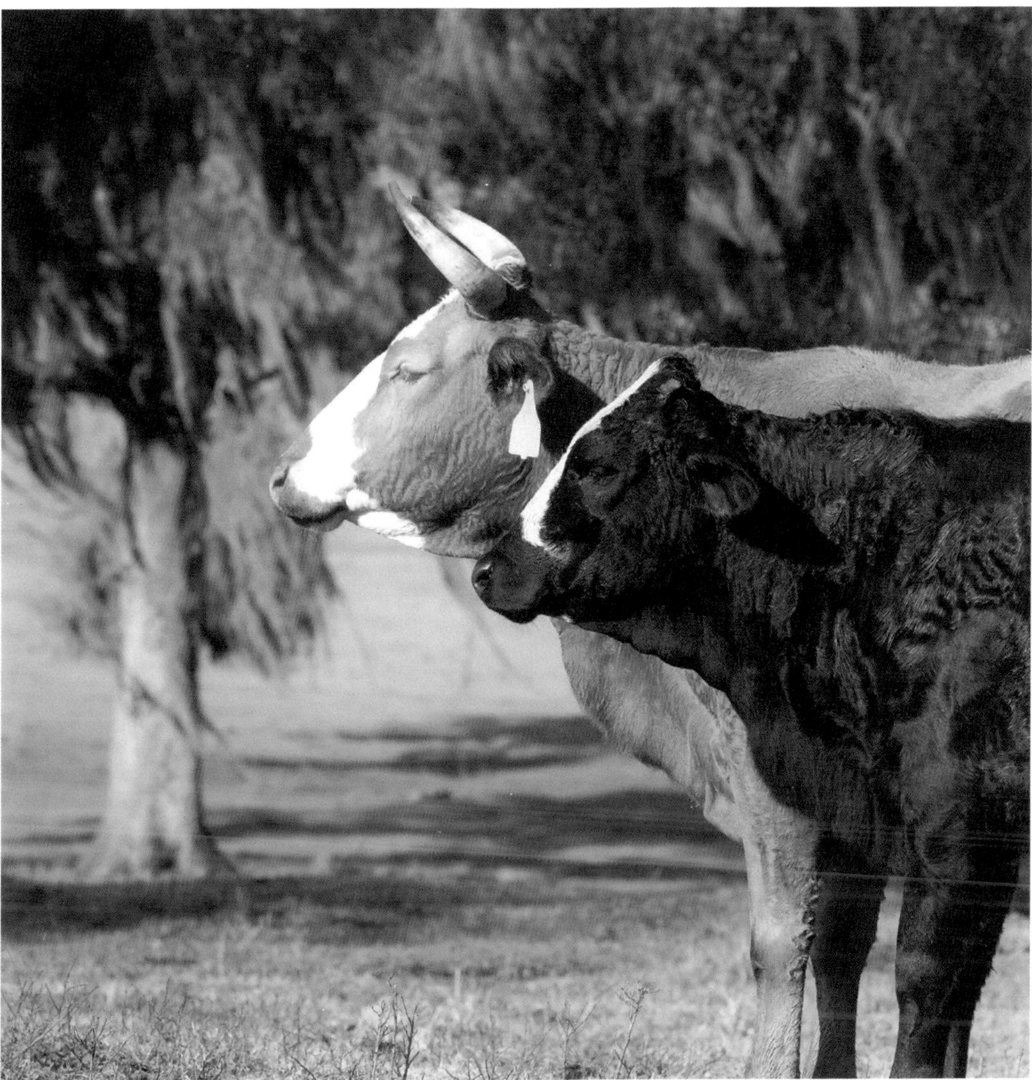

Ember *(Brangus mix) and* ***Burnadette*** *(Brangus mix)*

Ember was rescued in a group of forty cows from an extreme cruelty situation. She arrived in a sanctuary pregnant with Burnadette. See "Sunrise Moos: The Tale of a Rescued Herd" on page 113.

Note that the spelling of Burnadette's name is intentional. The sanctuary founders named Ember to fondly honor her fiery personality and continued the fire theme when her daughter was born.

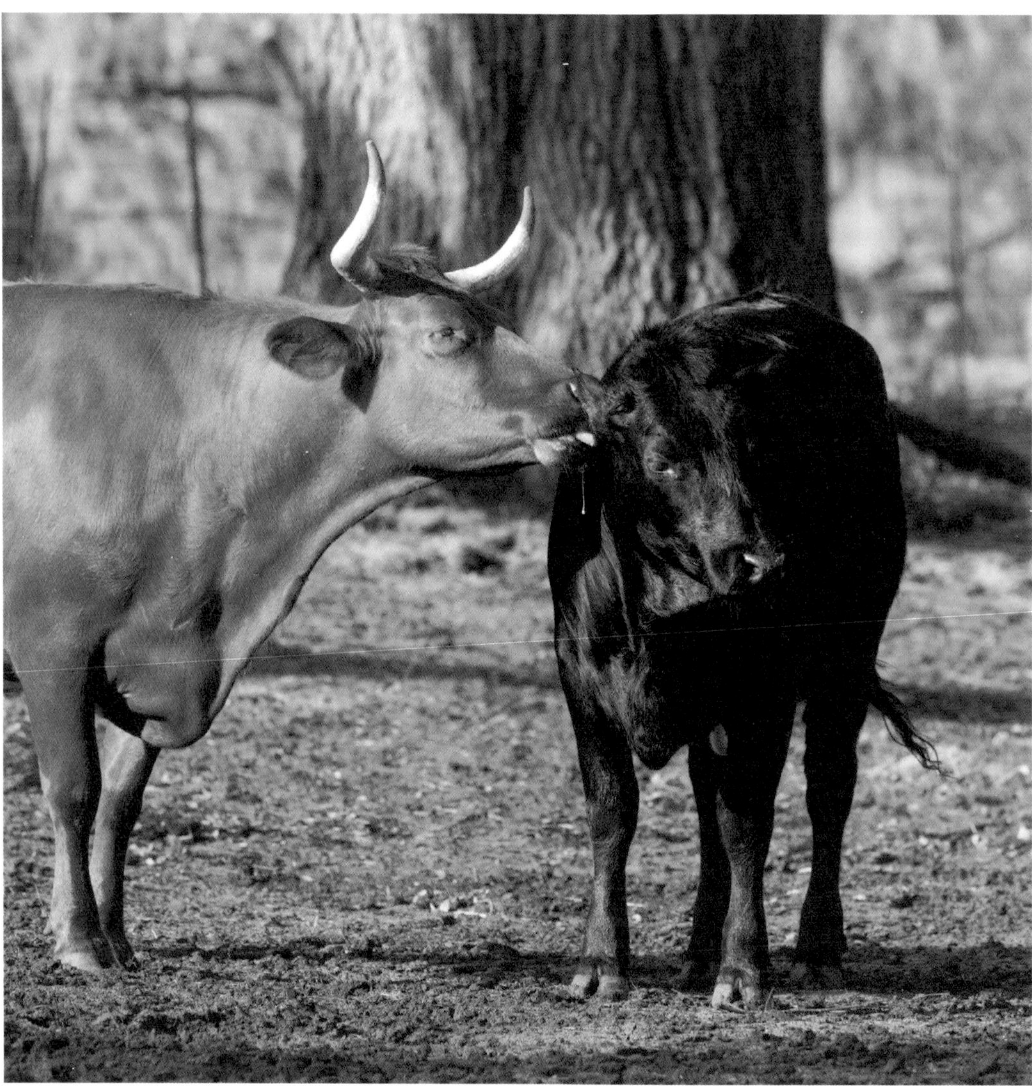

Dora Jean *(Dexter) and* ***Terri*** *(Dexter)*

Dora Jean was rescued in a group of forty cows from an extreme cruelty situation. She arrived in a sanctuary pregnant with Terri. *See "Sunrise Moos: The Tale of a Rescued Herd" on page 113.*

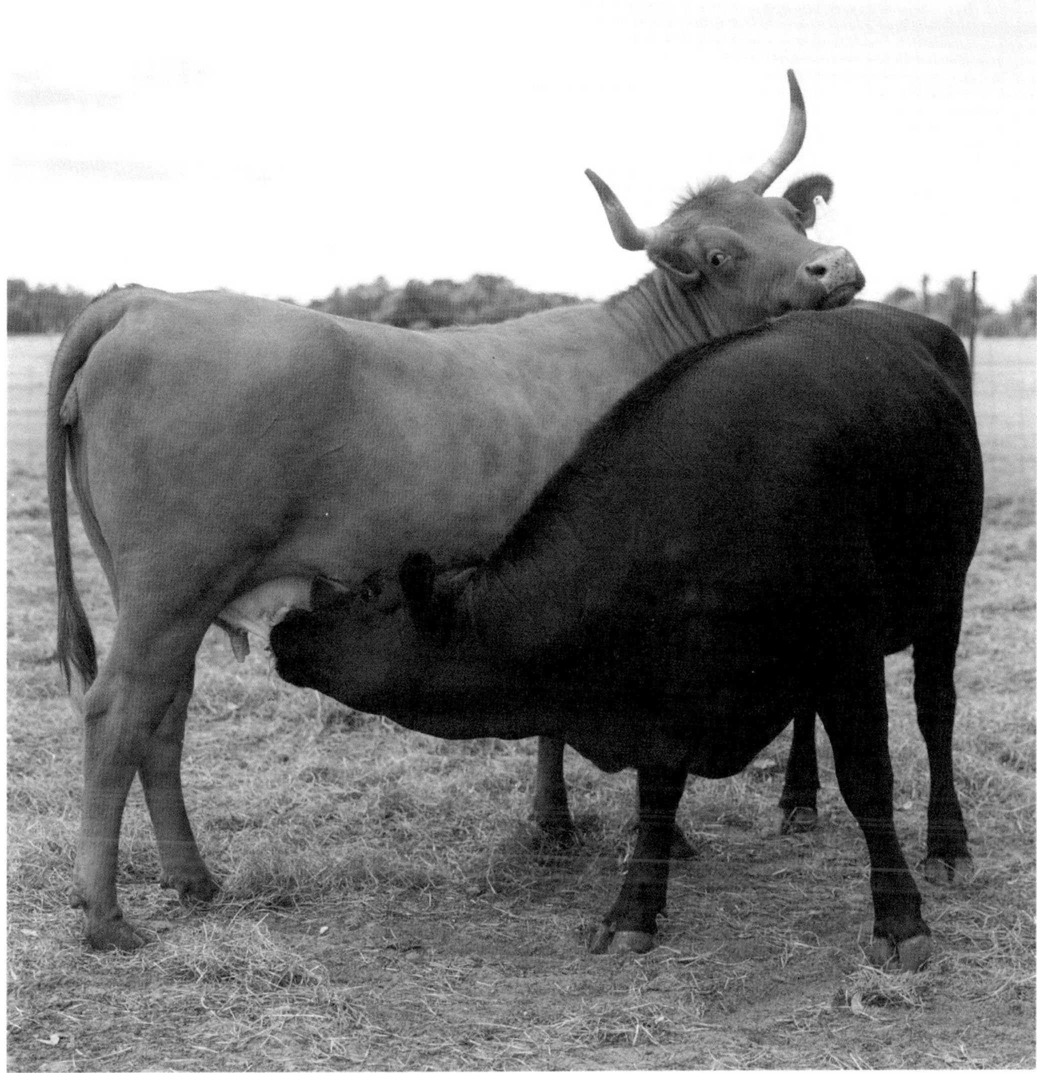

Dora Jean** and **Terri

When allowed, children of cows can nurse for several years, long after they have weaned themselves and rely on grass and hay for their nutritional requirements. This stage of nursing further strengthens the mother-child bond.

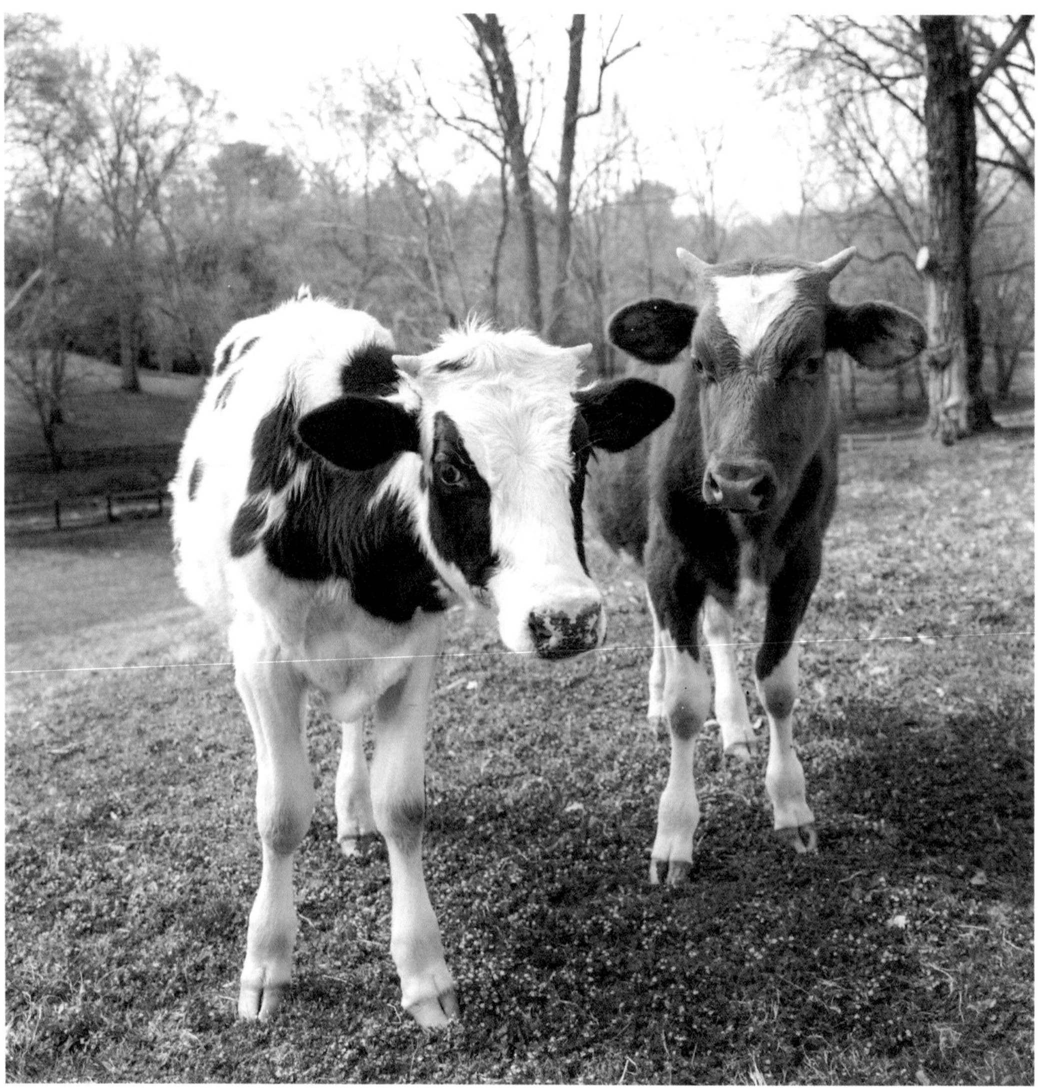

***Mickey** (Holstein) and **Moose** (Holstein)*

These steers were born on small dairy farms in Vermont. See "Mickey and Moose" on page 89.

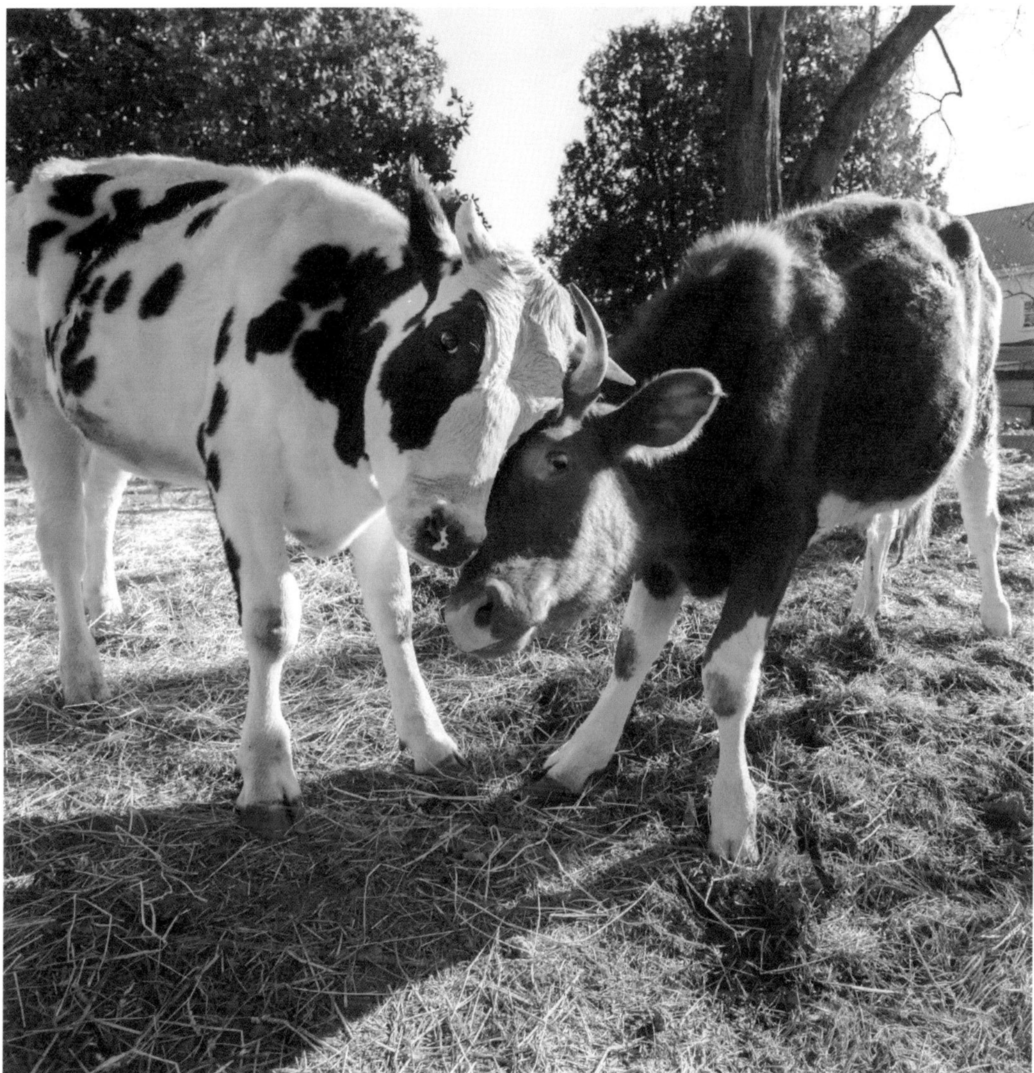

Mickey *and* ***Moose***

Moose is the more timid of the pair. Whenever a new visitor arrives, he often hangs back and waits for his best friend, Mickey, to make the introductions before coming over for attention.

CRITTER CREEK FARM SANCTUARY

By Erin Amerman, Founder
Gainesville, Florida

Sunrise Moos: The Tale of a Rescued Herd

(Photographs on pages 44, 56, 57, 66, 107, 108, and 109)

May 21, 2021, was a typical hot, early summer day in Florida. The humidity glistened on our faces as I drove Chris and myself through the fields of Critter Creek Farm Sanctuary, the buggy bouncing along over the uneven terrain. We were doing daily chores—conducting health checks, ensuring the fences were intact, removing toxic weeds from the fields, and just visiting with the moopeople.

Spotting an errant weed, I stopped the buggy and hopped out to pull it when I heard Chris mutter an expletive. He was staring at his phone with a frown.

"Laurie Waggoner just texted," he said wearily.

Laurie was the director of the South Florida SPCA Horse Rescue, an organization based out of Homestead, Florida. Generally, a text from her meant that they had intervened in another cruelty case and had animals they needed to place.

I repeated Chris's expletive. "Another cruelty case?"

Chris nodded. "They just rescued forty cows."

I groaned as I silently calculated how many of the rescued cows we could accommodate. Maybe five? Six? "What do you think? Can we take some of them?" I asked, flinging the weed into the back of the buggy.

"Look at the photos," Chris said grimly, handing me his phone.

What I saw broke me in ways I hadn't realized I could still be broken after so many years of rescue work. Since Critter Creek's founding in 2016, we had taken in animals from many cruelty cases. Some animals had arrived thin, others had been physically abused, and still others had suffered medical neglect. But none of that prepared me for the photos Laurie had sent. These cows were skeletal. The animals looked like walking corpses—skin and bones, with lifeless eyes. I honestly hadn't realized that an animal could be so emaciated and remain living.

As I waded through Laurie's photos, I read her texts to get the full story. The SFSPCA and law enforcement had raided a property in Sunrise, Florida. The 125-acre lot had no grass for grazing. No one was feeding the cows. The animals relied on irregular rainfall for water. For months, they had withered away as concerned neighbors repeatedly reported the property owner to the authorities. It wasn't until a good Samaritan photographed dead and dying cows on the property that law enforcement finally intervened.

When the authorities finally arrived, they found corpses littering the fields in varying stages of decay. Some cows had given birth but were unable to make milk to feed their babies. These babies survived only by the grace of other mother cows in the herd who were able to make milk, and who graciously shared their supply with them. Forty moopeople had managed to survive. Many hadn't.

I felt dizzy as my mind processed what they had suffered—the pains of starvation as they grew smaller with each passing day; the longing for water as they became parched in the Florida heat; and the distress they experienced as they watched their friends and family suffer the same fate, being powerless to help them. Cows are herd animals. They form strong, lifelong bonds with their family members, just like we do. They form best friendships, just like we do. And to imagine these animals helplessly witnessing their friends and family members starvng to death while they themselves also slowly wasted away? Their suffering, their loss, was palpable. It was crushing. Right then and there, I was determined that they would suffer no more losses.

Choking back a sob, I handed Chris back his phone. "Tell Laurie we will take the whole herd. These animals will not be separated. They will not lose any other family members or friends." Chris nodded silently and sent the message to Laurie. And just like that, our herd grew by forty cows whom we dubbed the "Sunrise Moos."

* * *

Cases like this raise the question of *why*. Why in the world would a farmer starve his animals? Simply from an economic standpoint, it doesn't appear to make sense. Wouldn't emaciated animals fetch a lower price at auction? The answer, surprisingly, is no.

Healthy female cows are purchased at auction to be breeders. These cows fetch a lower price because they still require some investment by a farmer. Sick, skinny cows, on the other hand, are purchased at auction to be "cull cows" that are sent straight to slaughter. Because they require no additional investment, they actually fetch a higher price. Buyers for fast food restaurants are infamous for purchasing cull cows because the quality of the animals' "meat" is not important to such establishments.

* * *

The Sunrise Moos arrived at Critter Creek a few weeks after their initial rescue. As they stepped off the trailer, I walked among them to assess their condition and begin giving them names. Their state was grim—bones jutted out at unnatural angles. Many were covered in horrific brands. And they were so terrified that my initial walkabout quickly devolved into chaos as the animals' anxiety spiked. Some cows, like Felicia and Annie, fled in terror. Others, like Patsy, attempted to jump the fence. Still others, like Nova and Miriam, put their heads down and hoofed the ground to tell me to back off. I quickly learned to hug the fence lines when walking in their area, which minimized their stress. I also learned to always come bearing gifts of food and treats.

Although their fear was predictable—they had only ever experienced cruelty at human hands—some of their behavior was surprising. Lola was unexpectedly friendly. Sparrow, who was so weak she could barely stand, was also quite bold. Amie was cautious but also curious. And when our vet visited to do their initial health screening and vaccines, we discovered that the Sunrise Moos had another surprise for us.

Rescuing animals who are seen as mere commodities comes with certain quirks. These are creatures who are considered to have value only when they're producing something—milk, eggs, or baby animals to sell. As a result, when rescuing farmed animals, there's a good chance at least a few will arrive pregnant. So, when we took in the Sunrise Moos, we assumed at least a couple would be expecting babies. But when our vet examined them, he found that "a couple" was actually ten. Our forty-cow rescue instantly turned into a fifty-cow rescue. While this was daunting, we also looked at it as a gift. These babies would be born into sanctuary, and never have to suffer like their parents. They would know only peace, respect, and security.

The baby boom began in August of 2021 and continued through January of 2022. All were born healthy, save for Mo, who was born a little prematurely. But within a week, Mo and his mom, Celeste, were thriving. We hoped that these happy, carefree babies would help heal the whole herd, and our wish was granted. With each birth, the weight of the trauma carried by the herd seemed to lessen, and eventually the adults frolicked along with the babies.

Three years after their rescue, the Sunrise Moos are almost unrecognizable. They are healthy, happy, and calm. I can walk among them with no risk of it devolving into chaos—my only real fear is being stepped on by an overly friendly mooperson who doesn't know her size. Some of them still don't like us (Nova and Miriam, I'm looking at you). But that's okay. They know they are safe, and that's what's important.

The Sunrise Moos are a remarkable case study in the lives of cows. Their story illustrates cows' incredible resilience and their capacity for forgiveness. Forty animals who had suffered unimaginably are now happy and content. And ten babies who would have been born into horrific conditions will never experience what their parents did.

This is rescue. This is sanctuary.

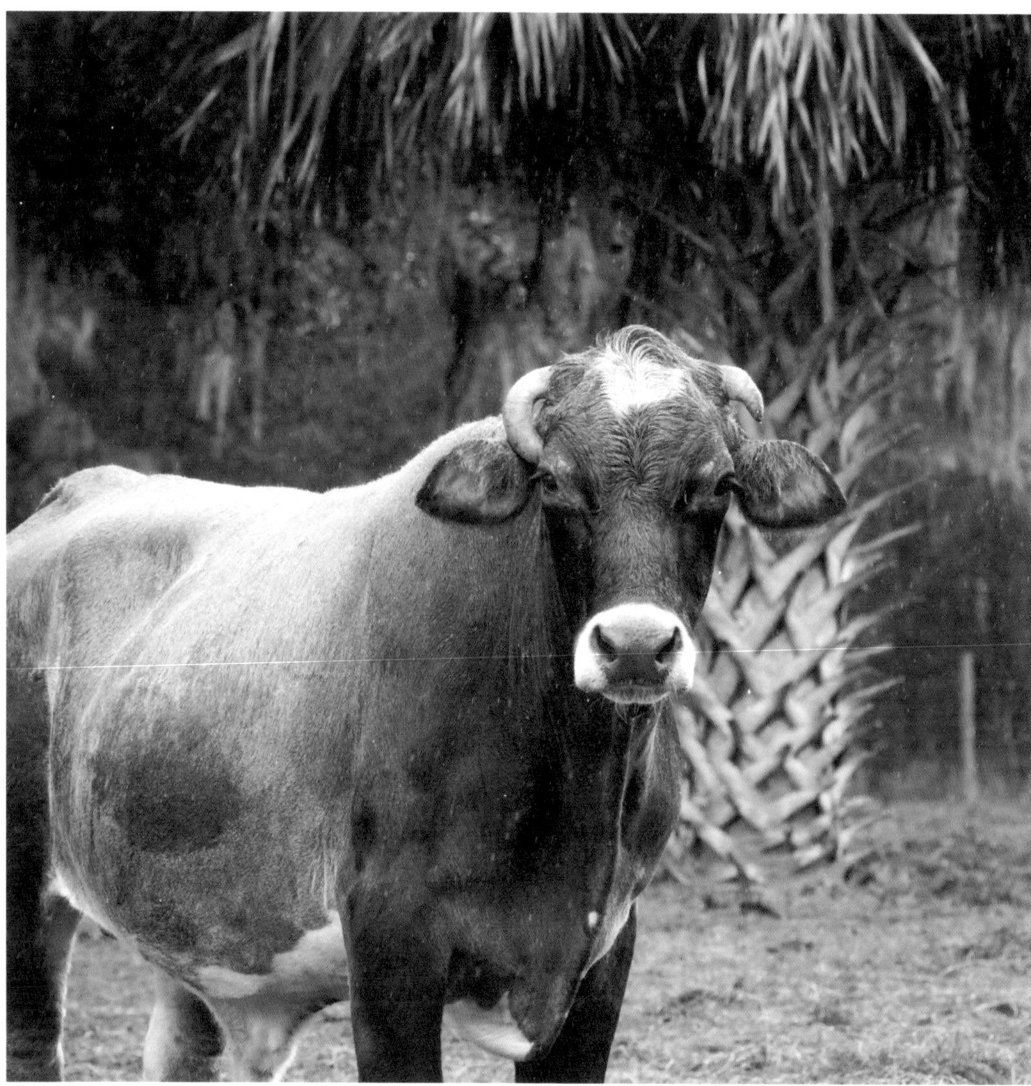

Otis *(Jersey mix)*

Otis and his family were seized by the South Florida SPCA from a cruelty case that left them emaciated. Otis and his children, Iggy and Violet, arrived together. Otis is a gentle, caring father, who grooms and lies beside his children.

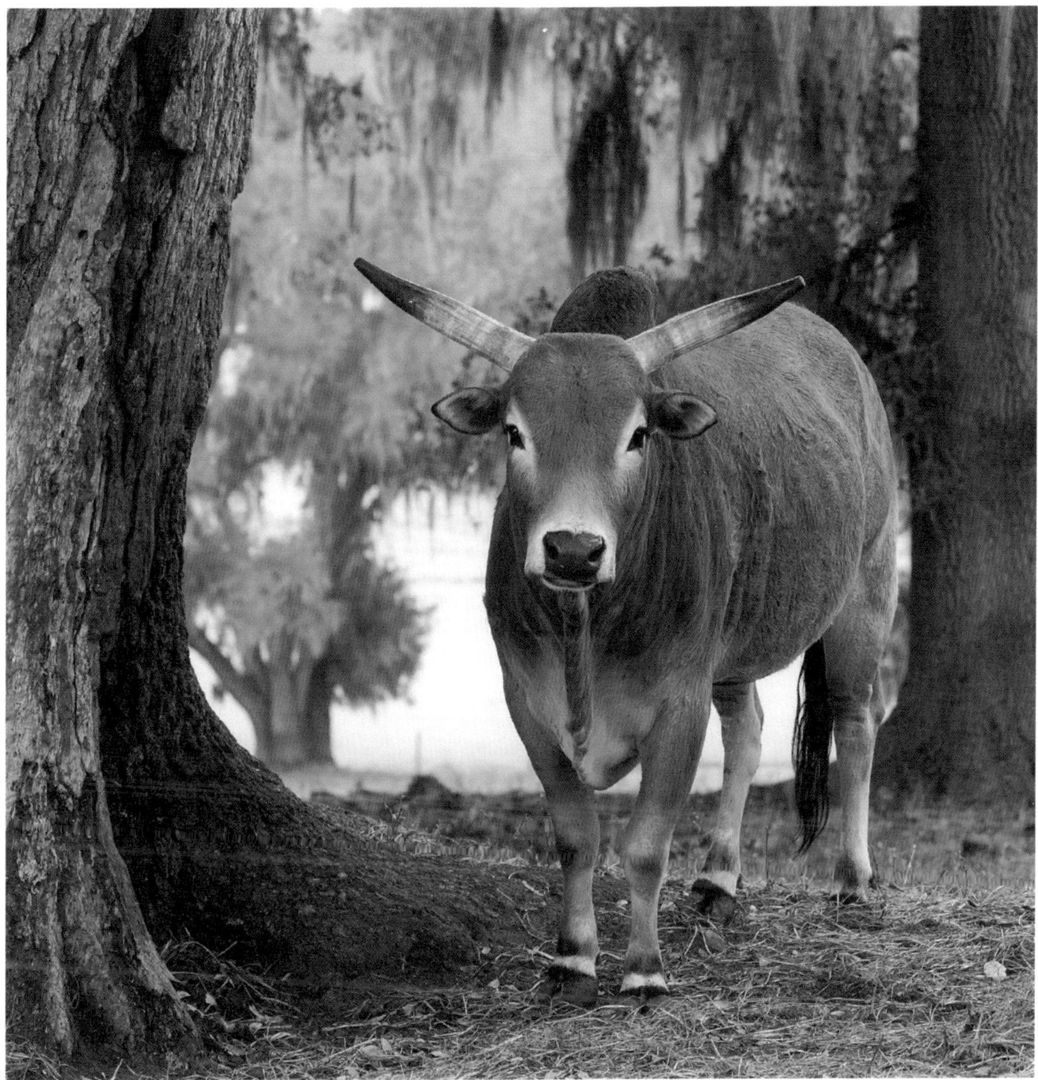

Tony *(Zebu)*

An elderly couple rescued Tony as a baby. When the husband's health declined, they were no longer able to care for their cows.

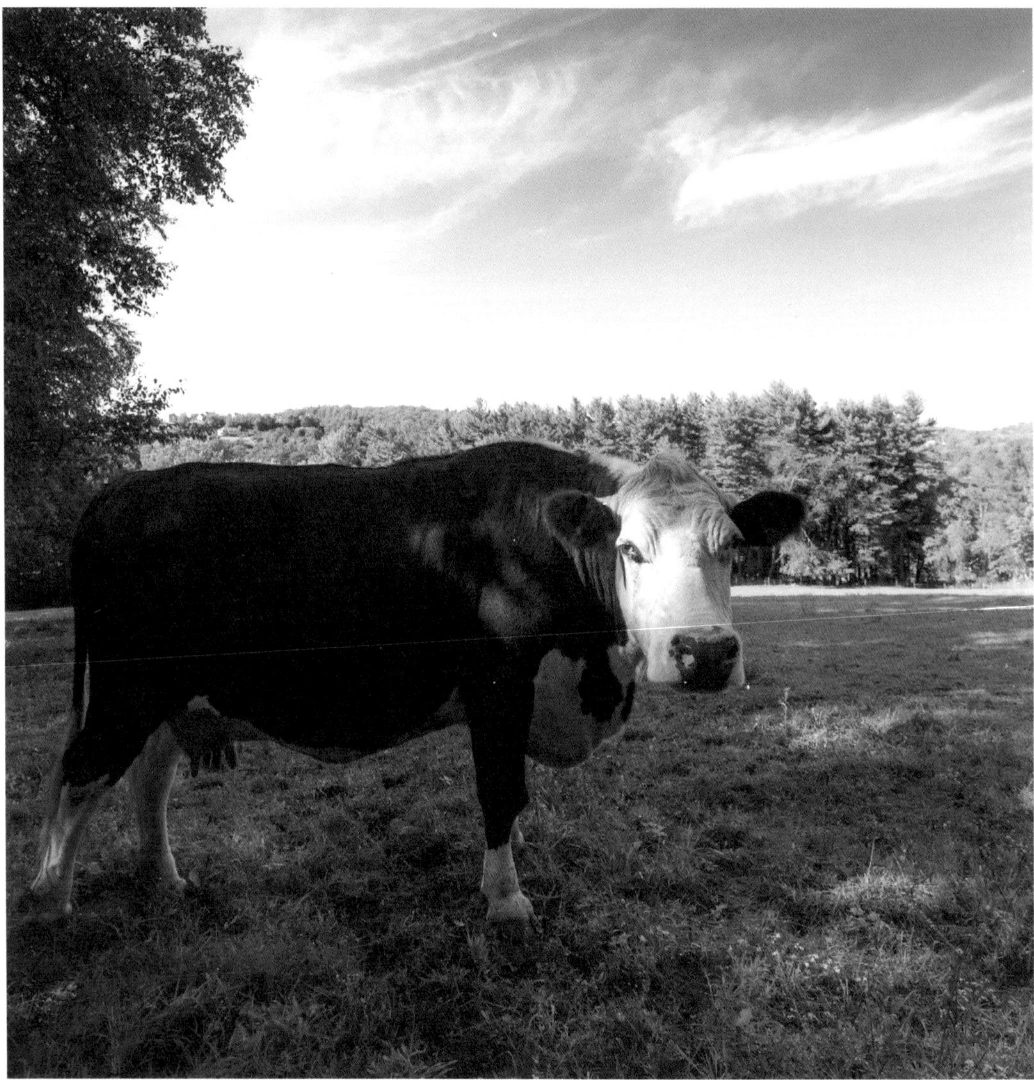

***Ethel** (Holstein/Hereford cross)*

A couple ran a small dairy farm. After the husband passed away, the wife sold the land and all their other cows but was fond of Ethel and Surprise and wanted them to remain together. *See "Ethel and Surprise" on page 49.*

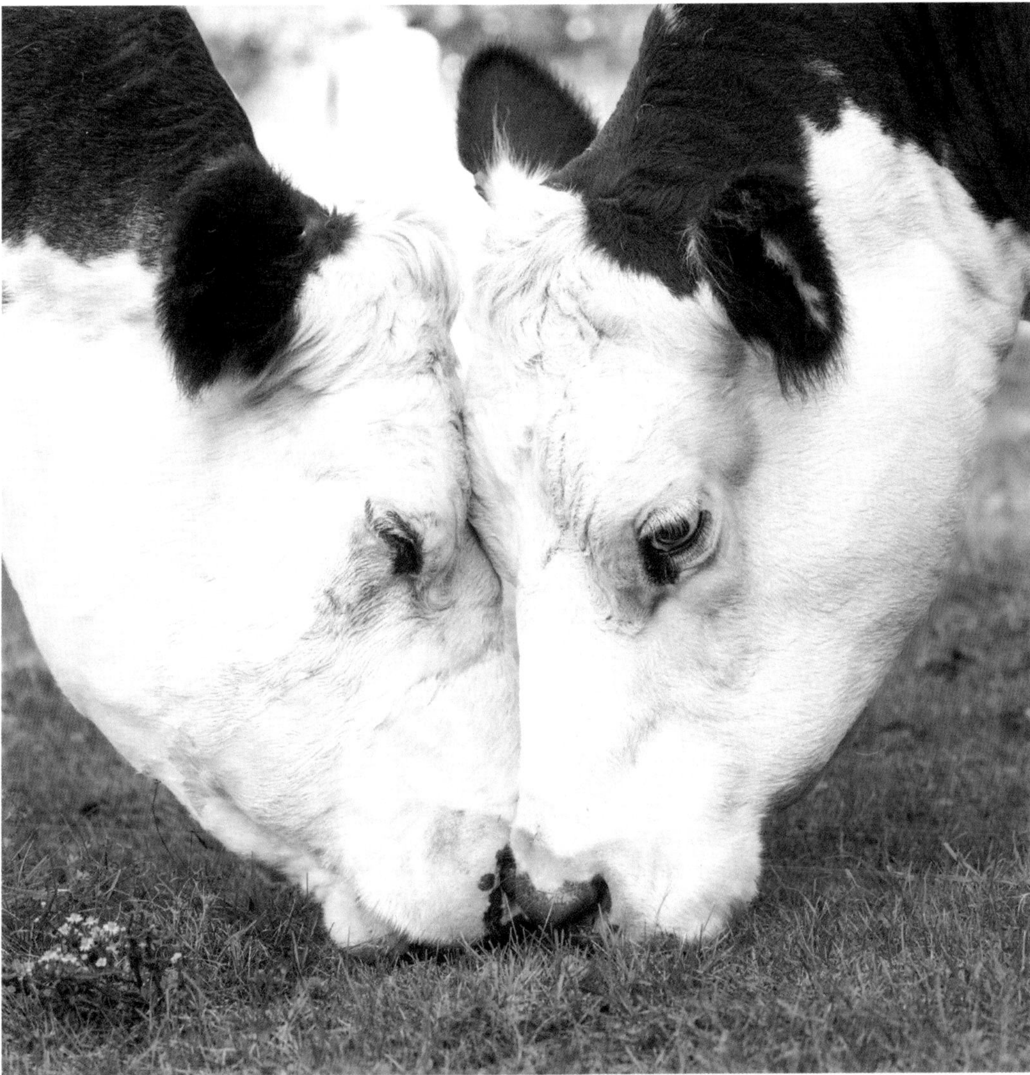

Ethel *and* ***Surprise*** *(Holstein/Hereford cross)*

Although Ethel and her daughter, Surprise, are now over twenty-three and seventeen years old, respectively, they have as close a relationship as ever. They frequently caress each other and nap together.

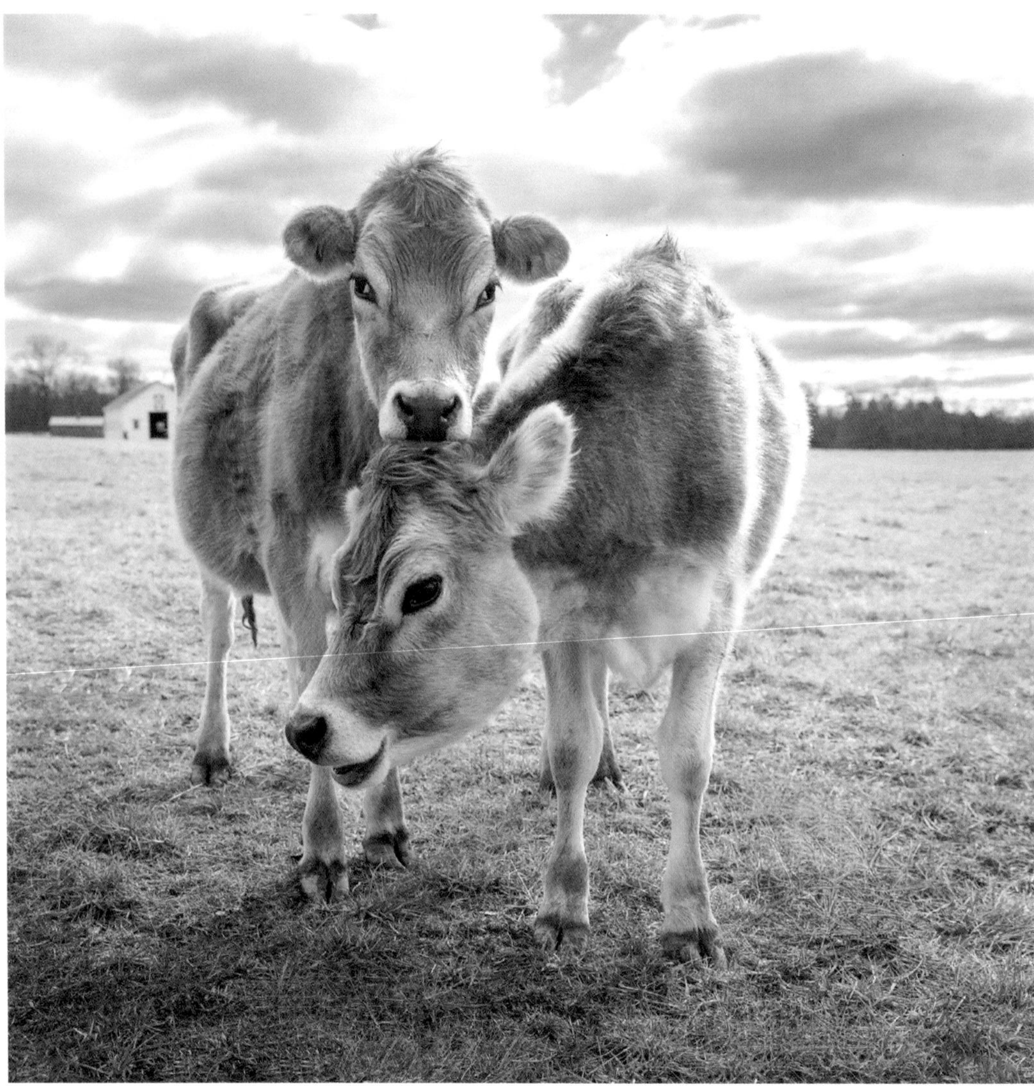

***Richie** (Jersey) and **Romeo** (Jersey)*

These steers were seized, along with goats and sheep, from a farm on which they were neglected and starving.

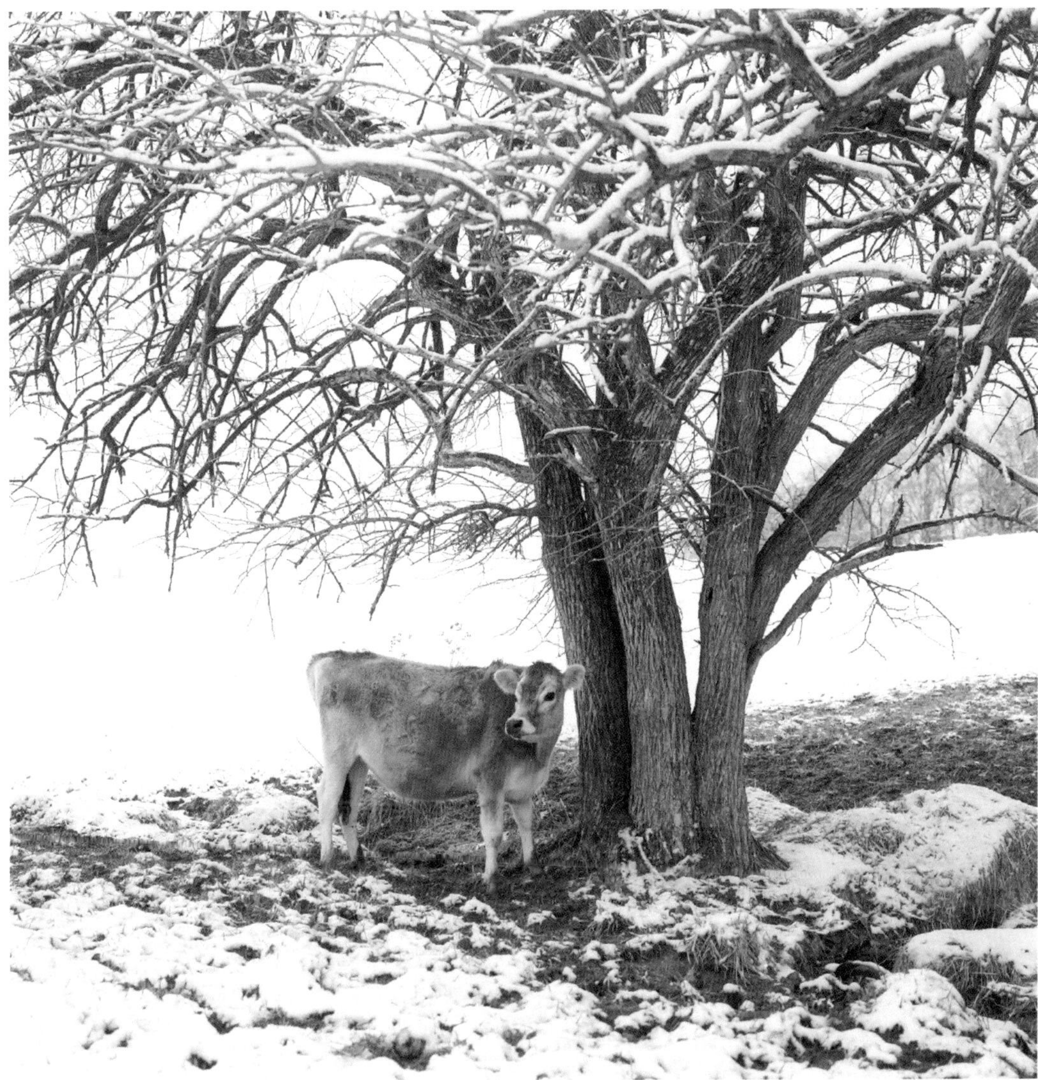

Richie

Richie and his best friend, Romeo, love to explore the acres of grassland and woods available to them. But they always return to the herd and caress each other before lying down together.

POPLAR SPRING ANIMAL SANCTUARY

By Terry Cummings, Founder
Poolesville, Maryland

Maple and Grayson

(Photographs on pages 84 and 85)

Living on a farm surrounded by cows seemed like a dream come true when we first began renting a historic house on 400 acres, where the adjacent land was leased to a beef cattle farmer. Little did we know that these cows would change our lives.

Every morning, we woke to gentle mooing, and sat on the porch watching the young calves running and playing with abandon, their mothers calling to them when they strayed too far. They seemed to have an idyllic life, free to roam the entire farm with its rolling hills of open pastures, woods, and creeks. Over the next few months, we enjoyed getting to know many of them as individuals—we named them, and hand fed them apples. We spent hours just watching them and were surprised to observe that the cows had social groups very similar to humans. The mother cows would go off to graze together in small friend groups, while the young females (we imagined these to be the "teenagers") babysat the calves, who spent hours playing and chasing each other, just like small children. There were over a hundred cows, but if one calf cried out, that baby's mother came running instantly to check on her youngster. Each mom absolutely knew her own baby's voice; it was amazing. These cows had a wonderful life—until they didn't.

If one of the cows had the misfortune to get sick or slip and fall, the farmer would never call a veterinarian, instead leaving them to suffer and slowly die. We called our local animal control service to report him but were told that farm animals are exempt from the anti-cruelty laws in every state—they refused to even investigate the incidents. We did the best we could to help the ailing cows but were limited; it was heartbreaking. And then one day, a huge trailer arrived. Men with electric prods forced the cows onto the trailer and drove them to a slaughterhouse. We were devastated by the treatment and ultimate fate of the beautiful animals we had grown to know and love, and it had a profound effect on us. We became vegan, and in 1997 started Poplar Spring Animal Sanctuary to rescue and provide a permanent home for formerly abused and neglected cows and other farm animals.

One of our most memorable rescues was Maple, a sweet Jersey cow who spent her entire life chained inside a barn, being milked daily as an Amish family's only cow. Every year, she was bred so that she would have a baby and produce more milk, only to have that calf taken away as soon as they were born, so that all of her milk could go to the family. When she was only seven years old, they decided to replace her with another, younger cow, and planned to butcher her on the farm—even knowing that she was nine months pregnant. Thankfully, a kind woman who met Maple while visiting there talked the family into letting her go to a sanctuary instead.

When Maple arrived at Poplar Spring, we were shocked at her appearance. We had never seen a cow so emaciated. The vet scored her Body Condition Score a two on a one-to-nine scale. It was impossible to think that she was about to give birth, but only four days later, baby Grayson was born. He was thankfully healthy, and Maple immediately became a doting mother, grooming and nursing him constantly, so happy that she was able to finally keep her baby. When Grayson was just one day old, Maple led him over to the fence separating her pasture. The other rescued cows were fascinated and mooed loudly—everyone came running to see the new baby, excitedly leaping and jumping around when they spotted the new arrival. They tried to lick and sniff Grayson through the fence while Maple proudly stood by, seeming to enjoy showing off her newborn. It took some time for Maple to trust us, and she was still worried that people would steal her baby, as had happened so many times before.

For the first few weeks, we often found tiny Grayson covered in hay, as if Maple had tried to hide him. And although she was proud to show him off to other cows, she did not want humans to touch him or come near him. She would anxiously try to push us away if we tried to pet him. Slowly, over time, she relaxed and realized that people could be good and kind, and that nobody would ever take her baby again. When Grayson was several weeks old, we introduced him and Maple to the rescued cow herd, who welcomed them immediately. They became one big family.

Grayson is now five years old, and he and Maple still spend much of their time together, grazing and strolling through the sanctuary's large pastures and fields, wading through creeks, and eating leaves in the woods. We are so happy we can provide Maple and Grayson with such a wonderful life, where they will be loved and cared for, and will always be together. We wish that all cows could live this way.

CAN WE READ A COW'S MIND?

Exploring Measures of Positive and Negative Emotions

Dr. Helen Lambert, BSc Hons, MSc, PhD
United Kingdom

Cows are herd animals, so communicating how they feel to one another is critical for navigating and succeeding in their social interactions. In my career as an animal welfare scientist, I have spent years exploring whether humans can learn to decode the movements and facial expressions of cows to reliably tell how they are feeling. Knowing whether a cow is feeling happy or sad can help us ensure that we give them the best in life. After all, despite our best efforts, we humans do not always know what is best for animals—they often have their own ideas!

At the start of my research journey with cows, I sought to test different measures of positive emotions, specifically looking at ear postures, eye whites, and nasal temperatures as prospective candidates for helping me to "speak cow." For this, I had the enviable job of making cows feel happy—I got to stroke cows for a living! Now, not all cows want to be stroked, so I do not recommend you run up to a herd of cows offering them a cuddle. But, once they get to know you, cows are highly affectionate animals.

In fact, I developed a very special bond with one of the cows in our research group. Poppy elected herself to be a part of the research group, as she made it very clear she was a huge fan of being stroked and would not take no for an answer. During the study, Poppy and I developed a particularly strong bond, and she would regularly seek me out for strokes. Then, during our very serious research sessions where I would stroke Poppy for five minutes at a time, she would often fall asleep with her head across my lap, a little like an oversized Labrador. Others in our team also developed their own bonds with specific cows, and we had to tailor data collection accordingly. Some cows simply showed stronger affection toward specific people, just like they do with one another.[1]

Poppy and the other cows in the group helped us to collect some fascinating data too, but this was only stage one, so first, let me explain what else we did. When we talk about emotional states, one way to categorize them is to separate them into positive and negative states (valence). Emotions also vary in terms of how aroused the individual is, and an emotion can be associated with a high or a low level of arousal.[2] When we stroked the cows, we elicited a positive, low arousal state—as evidenced by the fact that they often fell asleep during the experience. In stage two, we sought to elicit a high-arousal positive emotional state of excitement and a high-arousal negative emotional state of frustration. Please note the experience of frustration was only short-lived, and we considered it a cow-friendly alternative to eliciting other negative emotions such as fear or pain.

To do this, we conditioned the cows to expect the delivery of their usual feed when we rang a bell. This was nothing exciting for the cows; some ate it, and some did not. It was not big news. Then, once they associated the bell with this rather unexciting event, we mixed things up. Instead of their usual feed, we gave them highly desirable "concentrates." Concentrates are a high-energy feed that cows love, so the cows got excited. Now we know this, as we also measured their heart rates in this part of the study. Then, after a period of doing this, we changed things again. This time, upon the bell, instead of the concentrates, we gave the cows inedible woodchips. This was intended to induce frustration, and we could see from their heart rates and behavior that it worked.

Over the two phases, we elicited three different categories of emotions: a positive, low-arousal emotion (relaxed/calm) through stroking, a positive, high-arousal emotion (excitement) through the delivery of highly appetitive feed, and a negative, high-arousal emotion (frustration) by thwarting their expectations and giving them inedible woodchips. We could now determine whether the cows showed consistent changes across our measures in response to the different emotional states. Doing so would indicate that cows reliably express their emotions through their ears, noses, or eyes.

We worked with Holstein and Friesian cows who have highly mobile ears, and so we had an inkling that this was not purely a decorative feature. Given that they are highly social animals who spread out across the pasture, ears are perfectly placed to communicate attention and potentially also emotional experiences across the herd. Our results certainly suggest this may be the case. In particular, we found that cows perform certain, more

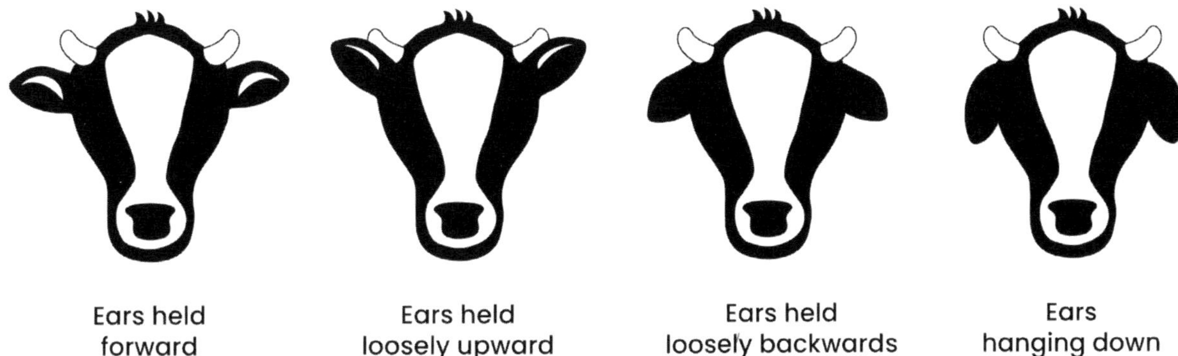

relaxed ear postures for longer when they are in a positive and calm emotional state from being stroked and that one ear posture in particular, a floppy perpendicular posture, is particularly characteristic of this state, as it was not performed at any other time.[3]

Conversely, when they are excited, we found that cows tend to spend more time in an upright ear posture and in a forward-facing ear posture when they are frustrated.[4]

Now, this isn't to say that if a cow has her ears facing forward, she must be feeling frustrated or some other negative, high-arousal state. Instead, ear postures in cows are about looking at the whole activity budget—how much time the cow has spent in that ear posture compared with others. Therefore, ear postures may reflect short-term emotional states and potentially longer-term moods.

The other two measures we looked at were more physiological. The amount of eye white a cow has visible at any one time varies depending on how much they tighten or relax the muscles around the eye. We found that both the high-arousal states of frustration and excitement led to increased visible eye white as the cows widened their eyes to take in more information about the exciting food, or lack of it.[5] Then, when we stroked the cows, they showed far less eye white[6]—not surprising considering that there is no visible eye white in a sleeping cow!

We also took the cows' nasal temperatures. Don't worry, we didn't stick a thermometer up their noses—we used an infrared thermography gun to do it remotely. The idea behind this is that when an animal is in fight or flight mode (a high-arousal state), blood is drawn away from peripheral areas like the nose to fuel core organs like the heart and lungs, which causes a drop in temperature in the peripheral regions. However, we wanted to know whether the emotion's valence (pleasantness or unpleasantness) had any effect on the nasal temperature, so we compared the temperatures across the three types of emotions.

Interestingly, regardless of arousal levels, all three emotional states (relaxed and calm, excitement, and frustration) elicited a drop in nasal temperature.[7] This rather confusing result goes to show how challenging this area is. It may be that nasal temperatures are reflective more of a change in emotional state, from positive to negative or neutral to positive, rather than being a reliable indicator of different emotions. The research is still a work in progress, as cows, like us, are complicated animals, so why should they make it easy for us to tell how they are feeling just by taking their temperature?

Ear postures provided the most concrete evidence of the three measures we explored. This is not surprising, since similar findings have been found with sheep, and since my research, other scientists have explored ear postures in cows in response to different stimuli to see how consistent ear postures are.[8] Overall, there are some promising outputs, which could one day be translated into a helpful tool to check in to see how a cow is feeling.

My research is part of a wider body of research into the minds of cows that continues to grow. Research that shows how cows form strong bonds with one another, specifically with one or two "besties,"[9] or that cows get excited when they learn something new (fondly nicknamed the "eureka effect"),[10] as well as more research that seeks to find ways in which we humans can learn to speak cow.[11] Progress is being made, and fellow scientists have found that in addition to the ears, cows may also show clear expressions of emotions through their entire face.[12] We just have to look more closely to see them.

Throughout my research, I have been lucky to form deep connections with the cows themselves, forging bonds that I will never forget. These sentient beings all have their own unique personalities, and as a result, they each form different bonds with different individuals. For me, Poppy stood out from the herd, seeking me out and pushing her way into my life and my heart. Scientists are meant to be objective, but when working with emotional, intelligent, sentient animals like cows, the heart has a firm role to play, too.

As we learn more about animals, our capacity to respect their needs improves. By learning to "speak cow," we can better ensure their well-being and improve their quality of life, acknowledging that, just as with humans, their perspectives and needs are diverse and deeply personal. Scientific research has shown that true animal welfare extends beyond physical health, encompassing the emotional and social dimensions that make each cow a unique individual.

ACKNOWLEDGMENTS

Gratitude flows naturally from the heart when we realize everything we've accomplished was only possible with help from many others.

In the spirit of a kid blowing on a dandelion, watching the seeds carry wishes into the wind, I offer heartfelt thanks to all those who've supplied the breeze to set this book aloft.

To all my cow teachers: Alexander, Juliet and Clifford, Moses, Nova, Petey and so many more. The more I learn, the more I realize how little I know.

To Brian Normoyle, for seeing the potential of this book and offering it the best possible home at Lantern Publishing & Media, to Emily Lavieri-Scull, for the beautiful cover and book design, and to Jason Handley and April Rondeau for tidying the manuscript text.

To the devoted staff and volunteers of farmed animal sanctuaries: Your tireless care for animals in need, and your commitment to ensuring they can live their lives with dignity and respect, is an inspiring example of empathy in action. The sanctuary employees who welcomed me, wrote the narratives about their cow residents and introduced me to each member of the herd (while identifying the ones with a penchant for treating visitors as rough-and-tumble playmates) include the following: Christiane Moore and Maureen Pickel of Chenoa Manor; Erin Amerman, Chris Amerman, Sheena Drost, and Scott Drost of Critter Creek Farm Sanctuary; Indra Lahiri, Robin Olson, and Sarah Thornton of Indraloka Animal Sanctuary; Sarah Salluzzo, Jonina Turzi, and Jil Desso of Lancaster Farm Sanctuary; Kelly Nix and Nancy Matthews of Luvin Arms Animal Sanctuary; John Netzel of Peaceful Fields Sanctuary; Michele Waldman and Jason Bolalek of Rosie's Farm Sanctuary; Bill and Ellen Crain of Safe Haven Farm Sanctuary; and Anne Shroeder of Star Gazing Farm Animal Sanctuary.

Special thanks to Terry Cummings and Dave Hoerauf, whose impact has left hoofprints all over this book. At Poplar Spring Animal Sanctuary—the first sanctuary I'd ever visited—engaging with the resident animals led me directly to the truth that farmed animals roam on an emotional landscape similar to our own. Since embracing veganism, I've walked for hundreds of hours alongside the rescued animals, often seeking out the cow herd before daybreak. I'm forever grateful for the friendship and trust Terry and Dave have shown toward me.

To the early readers of this book's introduction, Jonathan Balcombe and Polly Webb: Thank you for the gift of your time and editing skills. Your encouragement, pointed questions, and on-the-mark suggestions streamlined and elevated the message of the story.

To Helen Lambert, for graciously writing the scientific essay for this book, based on her research into the complex emotional lives of nonhuman animals. Her findings reveal how we can treat our fellow earthlings with respect for their fundamental needs and innate desires.

To the many, many people who've planted seeds of compassion in my own life, starting with my dad, Dick, who grew up in a family of hunters but chose to hunt beauty with his camera instead; and my mom, Sandy, who never refused anyone in need of an ear or shoulder.

And above all to Alisa, my tireless reader and kindred spirit, who set me firmly on my heart's path. This book could not have happened without you. Your wise counsel, support, and encouragement have accompanied me at each step of this journey. Each time you read the text of this book, you lightly suggested at least three improvements that knocked my socks off. Sweetheart, I recall one week, when a decorative panel on your car cracked and was left hanging, and you ripped it off with your bare hands so I could drive to a sanctuary the next day rather than loan you my car for your dog training appointments. My *gosh*, but every day I'm grateful you said yes.

NOTES

Introduction

1. Lori Marino and Kristin Allen, "The Psychology of Cows," *Animal Behavior and Cognition*, 4(4; 2017): 474–498, https://dx.doi.org/10.26451/abc.04.04.06.2017.
2. Cornelia Flörcke, Terry E. Engle, Temple Grandin, and Mark J. Deesing, "Individual Differences in Calf Defence Patterns in Red Angus Beef Cows," *Applied Animal Behaviour Science* 139(3–4; July 2012): 203–8, https://doi.org/10.1016/j.applanim.2012.04.001.
3. "Bond Between Cow and Calf Grows Deeper When Suckling Is Allowed," Faculty of Land and Food Systems, accessed March 9, 2024, https://www.landfood.ubc.ca/bond-between-cow-and-calf-grows-deeper-when-suckling-is-allowed/; Marino, "The Psychology of Cows," 484; "What You Never Knew About Dairy," Animals Australia, accessed March 9, 2024, https://animalsaustralia.org/our-work/compassionate-living/what-you-never-knew-about-dairy/.
4. Mónica Padilla de la Torre, Elodie F. Briefer, Brad M. Ochocki, Alan G. McElligott, and Tom Reader, "Mother–Offspring Recognition via Contact Calls in Cattle, Bos Taurus," *Animal Behaviour* 114 (2016), https://doi.org/10.1016/j.anbehav.2016.02.004.
5. Amy Hatkoff, *The Inner World of Farm Animals* (Stewart, Tabori & Chang, 2009), 76; "Fascinating Cow Facts," The Hay Manager, accessed February 2, 2023, https://www.thehaymanager.com/cattle-and-cows-round-bale-hay-feeders/fascinating_cattle_facts/; Margo Hayes, "Understanding Cattle Behaviour on Small Farms," FarmStyle Australia, accessed February 2, 2023, https://www.farmstyle.com.au/news/understanding-cattle-behaviour-small-farms.
6. de la Torre, "Mother–Offspring Recognition via Contact Calls in Cattle, Bos Taurus"; Alexandra Green, Cameron Clark, Livio Favaro, Sabrina Lomax, and David Reby, "Vocal Individuality of Holstein-Friesian Cattle is Maintained Across Putatively Positive and Negative Farming Contexts," *Scientific Reports* 9(18468; 2019), https://doi.org/10.1038/s41598-019-54968-4.
7. "An HSUS Report: The Welfare of Animals in the Meat, Egg, and Dairy Industries," The Humane Society of the United States, https://www.humanesociety.org/sites/default/files/docs/hsus-report-welfare-animals-meat-egg-dairy-industry.pdf.

8. Refer to any number of books published in recent years, including Marc Bekoff, *The Emotional Lives of Animals: A Leading Scientist Explores Animal Joy, Sorrow, and Empathy — and Why They Matter* (New World Library, 2024); Hatkoff, *The Inner World of Farm Animals;* and Barbara J. King, *How Animals Grieve* (University of Chicago Press, 2014). Also see bestselling books like Jonathan Balcombe, *What a Fish Knows: The Inner Lives of Our Underwater Cousins* (Scientific American/Farrar, Straus and Giroux, 2017); Jane Goodall, *Through a Window: My Thirty Years with the Chimpanzees of Gombe* (Mariner Books/Houghton Mifflin Harcourt, 2010); and Jeffrey Moussaieff Masson, *The Pig Who Sang to the Moon: The Emotional World of Farm Animals* (Random House, 2008).
9. Hatkoff, *The Inner World of Farm Animals*, 84; Critter Creek Farm Sanctuary (@crittercreekfarmsanctuary), Instagram reel, November 28, 2023, https://www.instagram.com/reel/C0MmwiArDAS/; "Do cows grieve? Traffic brought to a standstill as herd of cattle desperately try to revive their friend killed by a car," Daily Mail, last updated November 3, 3015, https://www.dailymail.co.uk/news/article-3302174/amp/They-not-cowed-Traffic-brought-standstill-cattle-herd-desperately-try-revive-friend-lying-lifeless-road-hit-car.html; "'I've never seen it before': Farmer's tragic post about 'freak accident'," Yahoo News, accessed March 20, 2024, https://au.news.yahoo.com/never-seen-a-cow-cry-before-farmers-heartbreaking-realisation-goes-viral-024012520.html.

Can We Read a Cow's Mind? Exploring Measures of Positive and Negative Emotions

1. David Val-Laillet et al., "Allogrooming in Cattle: Relationships between Social Preferences, Feeding Displacements and Social Dominance," *Applied Animal Behaviour Science* 116(2–4; January 2009): 141–49, https://doi.org/10.1016/j.applanim.2008.08.005.
2. Michael Mendl, Oliver H. P. Burman, and Elizabeth S. Paul, "An Integrative and Functional Framework for the Study of Animal Emotion and Mood," *Proceedings of the Royal Society of Biological Sciences* 277(1696; 7 October 2010): 2895–904, https://doi.org/10.1098/rspb.2010.0303.
3. Helen S. Proctor and Gemma Carder, "Can Ear Postures Reliably Measure the Positive Emotional State of Cows?," *Applied Animal Behaviour Science* 161(October 2014): 20–7, https://doi.org/10.1016/j.applanim.2014.09.015.
4. Helen S. Lambert and Gemma Carder, "Positive and Negative Emotions in Dairy Cows: Can Ear Postures Be Used as a Measure?," *Behavioural Processes* 158(2019): 172–80, https://doi.org/10.1016/j.beproc.2018.12.007.

5. Helen S. Lambert and Gemma Carder, "Looking into the Eyes of a Cow: Can Eye Whites Be Used as a Measure of Emotional State?," *Applied Animal Behaviour Science* 186(2016): 1–6, https://doi.org/10.1016/j.applanim.2016.11.005.
6. Helen S. Proctor and Gemma Carder, "Measuring Positive Emotions in Cows: Do Visible Eye Whites Tell Us Anything?," *Physiology & Behavior* 147(2015): 1–6, https://doi.org/10.1016/j.physbeh.2015.04.011.
7. Helen S. Proctor and Gemma Carder, "Can Changes in Nasal Temperature Be Used as an Indicator of Emotional State in Cows?," *Applied Animal Behaviour Science* 184(2016): 1–6, https://doi.org/10.1016/j.applanim.2016.07.013; Helen S. Proctor and Gemma Carder, "Nasal Temperatures in Dairy Cows Are Influenced by Positive Emotional State," *Physiology & Behavior* 138(November 2015): 340–44, https://doi.org/10.1016/j.physbeh.2014.11.011.
8. Monica Battini, Anna Agostini, and Silvana Mattiello, "Understanding Cows' Emotions on Farm: Are Eye White and Ear Posture Reliable Indicators?," *Animals* 9(8; 2019): 1–12, https://doi.org/10.3390/ani9080477; Daiana de Oliveira and Linda J. Keeling, "Routine Activities and Emotion in the Life of Dairy Cows: Integrating Body Language into an Affective State Framework," *PLOS ONE* 13(5; 2018): 1–16, https://doi.org/10.1371/journal.pone.0195674.
9. Val-Laillet et al., "Allogrooming in Cattle: Relationships between Social Preferences, Feeding Displacements and Social Dominance".
10. Kristin Hagen and Donald M. Broom, "Emotional Reactions to Learning in Cattle," *Applied Animal Behaviour Science* 85(3–4; 25 March 2004): 203–13, https://doi.org/10.1016/j.applanim.2003.11.007.
11. de Oliveira and Keeling, "Routine Activities and Emotion in the Life of Dairy Cows: Integrating Body Language into an Affective State Framework"; Lilli Frondelius et al., "The Effects of Body Posture and Temperament on Heart Rate Variability in Dairy Cows," *Physiology & Behavior* 139 (2015): 437–41, https://doi.org/10.1016/j.physbeh.2014.12.002; Annika Lange et al., "Talking to Cows: Reactions to Different Auditory Stimuli During Gentle Human-Animal Interactions," *Frontiers in Psychology* 11(15 October 2020), https://doi.org/10.3389/fpsyg.2020.579346.
12. Kris A. Descovich et al., "Facial Expression: An Under-Utilized Tool for the Assessment of Welfare in Mammals," *Altex* 34(3; 2017): 409–29, https://doi.org/10.14573/altex.1607161; Suresh Neethirajan, "Happy Cow or Thinking Pig? WUR Wolf—Facial Coding Platform for Measuring Emotions in Farm Animals," *AI* 2(3; 2021): 342–54, https://doi.org/10.3390/ai2030021; L. Ginger et al., "A Six-Step Process to Explore Facial Expressions Performances to Detect Pain in Dairy Cows with Lipopolysaccharide-Induced Clinical Mastitis," *Applied Animal Behaviour Science* 264(2023): 105951, https://doi.org/10.1016/j.applanim.2023.105951.

HOW DO YOU FEEL ABOUT THIS BOOK?

Although a cow herd or two has accepted me as a nominal member, I'm still a human, artist, and writer. I care what you think. If the photographs and stories resonate with you, would you take a moment and leave me an honest review? Your review would help other people decide to read it for themselves and maybe also get some enjoyment from it.

Thank you.

ABOUT THE AUTHOR

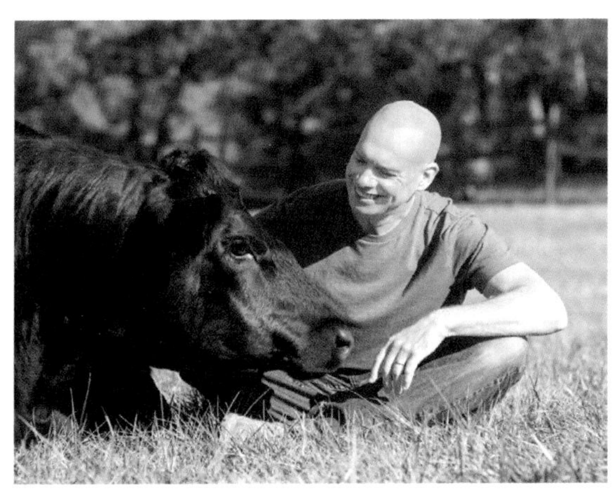

For over ten years, photographer Mark Peters has immersed himself in the everyday lives of the cow residents of farmed animal sanctuaries. He earns their trust by walking respectfully alongside the herd, coming to know each animal personally. Peters' ability to earn the trust of his portrait subjects has resulted in numerous cow licks, having his ear chewed on and getting chased (but never caught) by playful "puppy cows" on occasion. Peters lives in Maryland with his wife, Alisa, and the two little dogs who rule their home.

ABOUT THE PUBLISHER

Lantern Publishing & Media was founded in 2020 to follow and expand on the legacy of Lantern Books, a publishing company started in 1999 on the principles of living with a greater depth and commitment to the preservation of the natural world. Like its predecessor, Lantern Publishing & Media produces books on animal advocacy, veganism, religion, social justice, humane education, psychology, family therapy, and recovery. Lantern Publishing & Media is dedicated to printing in the United States on recycled paper and saving resources in its day-to-day operations. Lantern Publishing & Media titles are also available as e-books and audiobooks.

To learn more about Lantern Publishing & Media, please visit www.lanternpm.org.

facebook.com/lanternpm
instagram.com/lanternpm
tiktok.com/@lanternpmofficial